Secret Conversations

On Life, Love and Loss

Nigel Linacre

ISBN-13: 978-1517050207
ISBN-10: 1517050200

Contents

Secret Conversations

Also by Nigel Linacre

The Other Side of You

Knock, Knock, Who's God?

Why You Are Here – Briefly

The Magic of Existence

Why Men Don't Feel … And How They Can

Worry-Free Happiness

An Introduction to 3-Dimensional Leadership

The Successful Executive

Advertising for Account Handlers

Time and Again Life Poems

The Great War Poem

Leadership Paradoxes (co-author)

The Love and Loss of Connie and Ber (co-author)

Ground-Breaking (editor)

The Several Lives of Alberto Bioletti (editor)

Preface

These timeless conversations have lain hidden for a decade. They started when I wrote, "OK God, I am listening…" As soon as I consciously formed each statement in serif face, the response, here in arial typeface appeared instantly.

Each response felt like a gift, but was the gift just for me? Would the conversations resonate with others? I was cautious about sharing them, and kept them secret.

Reviewing unfinished projects this year, they stood out. I shared them with Margaretha Linacre, my father's wife, who read them and shared them with a Priest who shared them with … and I skimmed them again, and decided to publish. Somehow it feels right to let them go.

There's no need to take these conversations as the truth. They're just a truth, that came to me at a moment in time. If they resonate with you and help you find your truth, so much the better.

People talk to a God they may be imagining, in a crisis. These conversations started without a crisis, when I wrote …

1. Time to Tune in

OK God, I am listening. I have listened to myself for such a long time and heard little of much interest. I'd prefer to listen to you.

And why is that?

I should like to understand why I am here so I may fulfil any purpose I may have. I have a nagging sense that there is more, that I am missing something.

OK, where do you want to begin?

Let's start with why I am here.

You are here to express yourself.

Why here?

Here, there, it's all the same, you have to be somewhere.

And it's up to me how I express myself?

Yes it is.

OK, who am I?

You are an expression of the divine.

And that's you?

More or less, yes.

Am I mind, body or soul?

You are all of those things, some more temporarily than others, but think of yourself as something different.

What?

Energy.

OK, this is extraordinarily easy. I mean, this dialogue.

I am always here, always listening, always ready to respond.

So why do I spend so little time listening to you?

Because you have been trying to figure things out for yourself, and you cannot.

It feels like that is in my make-up, that I have to figure things out. I mean this is an amazing mystery you have got running here.

Spell it out.

Well, you have thousands of millions of human beings, not to mention millions of other species, and as for us, we are born, we live and we die, and though we sometimes wonder why, most of us don't seem to get anywhere, and those of us who give the impression of having got somewhere don't seem to be able to express it in ways that others understand.

And why don't the others understand?

I think it is because we have to change. We have to change in order to understand. In fact, that's the point.

Very good.

So where to from here?

As always, that is up to you.

Really, I am on my own again?

No, you are never on your own?

And how will I experience not being on my own?

The divine promptings are always present.

And how will I experience being on my own?

You cut yourself off, you are very good at that.

I would like to have you around a bit longer.

I've nowhere else to go.

Tell me more about the divine promptings, so it's really clear. How do I get them?

Think of it as being like a radio frequency. You have to tune in.

Why can't I hear it all the time?

You are set to the wrong station.

Why don't you make it easy for us to hear it all the time?

It is.

Why don't you make it so we are bound to get it all the time?

During wars, governments block certain frequencies. I don't do that. You can listen to what you choose. And you do.

OK, I choose you.

Occasionally.

Occasionally?

Yes, occasionally you choose me.

Fair point.

And when you have chosen me, what have you experienced?

It feels beautiful, wonderful, cosseted, held, loved, and yet all of this feels like the faintest rays of a bright sun. Also, and although my experience of choosing you is – I shall call it glorious – it satisfies some appetites, it doesn't satisfy others.

Like what?

Thirst, hunger.

I have laid on all these things for you.

I mean, physical contact doesn't feel like having a good physical meal. It feels different.

Because it is, and that's OK.

Yes, it is very OK. I get distracted.

Keep coming back.

Yes, I will.

If you want to.

I do. A metaphor occurs to me. Being in the world is like Mission Impossible with amnesia. I have this real sense of having been given a mission but not knowing what it is.

You do know.

What is it?

It is to make the way plain.

Plain and simple?

Yes, but it isn't quite correct to say it is your mission.

I thought you just said it was.

There are many way-makers. It isn't uniquely yours.

OK, fine. So what do I have to do to make the way plane.

Do what you are doing.

Listening.

Yes, and understanding.

And ...

Walking.

Walking?

Yes, you have to walk the way.

Now I am a little scared.

Because ...

I am apprehensive that you are going to tell me that I have to give up all my possessions.

You think you don't?

I do?

You will give them all up, pretty soon, when you pass out of this world. Did you think you can take them with you?

No, not for a minute. OK, so I can go some of the way, right now, in this lifetime, while I still have stuff, but in order to go all the way, I have to give everything up?

What do you think?

That sounds compelling: to be in heaven I have to stop being myself.

That's about it.

But I could stop being myself in this lifetime?

And aren't there moments when you have?

Yes, fleetingly. So I have to stop being me.

And start being me.

Really?

What did you think this was all about? Did you think there was a middle way between being you and being me?

But what if I want to stay me? What if I am not ready for the big surrender?

Then you will, but not for long.

I thought we had free will, and you've already implied we don't cease to be at the end of the life each of us is living.

That depends.

On whether we are good or bad?

No, on: Who you mean?

What do you mean?

Nigel Linacre has this life. And you know there aren't many Nigel Linacres.

That's just a label.

Nigel Linacre's body de-constitutes.

Well it is de-constituting – and re-constituting – all the time.

And it will stop re-constituting.

So what does continue?

The real you.

So my body isn't really me?

It is a temporary manifestation of you, like a suit of clothes.

OK.

As you are now.

I am a temporary manifestation of me!?

Of course, what else could you be?

I could be the manifester.

Bingo.

But there's more, isn't there, aren't there really three of us?

Explain how you see it.

There's the temporary manifestation of me, the manifester and the real me.

And the real me is?

The one who continues after this life

And?

Who preceded this life? Who always was and always will be, but that doesn't feel like who I am.

Because you are not.

In fact, I have been wondering if I should really be having this conversation.

Why ever not?

Because I am not worthy of it. And as I have been having this thought I thought I sensed my connection weakening.

You've said you want to be an effective spiritual teacher.

Yes, I admit it.

Why admit?

Because it is a big thing to own up to.

Can anyone be an effective spiritual teacher?

Yes, absolutely.

Including everyone who gets these words.

Yes, certainly.

And what do they have to do?

Turn up, tune in, listen out.

And then?

The way will be made plain.

Are you ready for this?

I think I am. Why does it sometimes seem pointless?

Because you lose the connection.

Why do I sometimes get carried away with myself and run up dead end alleys?

Because you lose the connection.

Why do I sometimes doubt?

Because you lose the connection.

OK, I get this, how do I lose the connection?

You get in the way.

Of what?

You get in the way of the way. Actually, you tune out.

And how do I do that?

You get distracted.

Can I explain a little bit about how this is happening?

I wish you would.

Well, it seems to me that I write something and then, whoosh, like a compressed data file, your answer is there. It also feels to like you give me little nudges as to what I should write.

On Life, Love and Loss

And how do you know the difference?

It is all a matter of feel. There is a lightness about all the stuff I feel nudged towards. As soon as words comes up, I can basically weigh them for lightness or heaviness and choose accordingly.

To know if it's alright, sense if it is light.

OK, so let's get back to the way.

There are light ways and dark ways.

Like right and wrong.

Simply like light and dark, and you can actually feel the difference. Right and wrong implies something else, namely judgement. And when you judge you don't love, and when you don't love, you aren't on the way, and when you aren't on the way you don't understand.

So I use my lightometer to perceive the way tending to what is light and avoiding what is dark.

Be aware of the light and the dark inside and around you, and constantly choose light.

I'll try.

And choose light for the darkness you encounter.

Please explain.

The brighter you are, the more relative darkness you may encounter, the more opportunities you have to share your light with them.

Years, ago, my two young sons were having a boisterous argument. I jumped in and told them to be quiet, but they persisted. Within seconds, three of us were squabbling. Looking back, I didn't make the light choice.

And how did it feel when you were squabbling?

It felt awful.

So darkness is pretty easy to recognise. Whenever you meet darkness with darkness, you simply compound the problem.

So when someone attacks you …

15

Be bright, as bright as you can be.

What happens to darkness when it meets the light?

It brightens up. It changes, it cannot not be changed, darkness is defenceless when it meets the light. Try switching on a light in a dark room.

It's that simple. It's black and white.

Yes, it's that simple. But developing any new capability may take time and practice.

How could one practice?

Anytime, anywhere, pay attention to how you are feeling be the observer of those feelings: light and dark, build the light feelings and let go of the dark ones. Any time, sense your inner turbulence or stillness and ask for calm. Anytime, sense the light around you, above you and below you and draw upon it. This will assist the process.

And?

And when you encounter darkness, be very aware. Notice that it is outside of you and that you don't have to let it in. If and when it does get in all you have to do is notice that it is darkness and let it go. It will pass.

I really feel we could go somewhere with this. I feel serene, yet I noticed something when I took time out just now. On seeing the mail on the mat my first thought was it would be trouble!

2. A Question of Will

OK: it's day two and I would like to tune in. I've had my quiet time and run my energy exercise.

Why don't you explain your energy exercise?

I imagine light coming down upon my crown, flooding down to the brow level, my throat, heart, root and down to my feet, and as I do that I chant a name for God, then I imagine or sense energy swirling down my left side and up my right a handful of times and then down my front and up my back.

And why do you do this?

I think it helps me to tune in. And another thing, I was nervous you wouldn't be here. In fact, how do I know it's you?

Do you know it's me?

No.

Then you don't. You are operating on trust, you are feeling your way, and that's how it is.

Wouldn't it be easier if I could access you through some group, say a religion, where we could all confirm to one another that we are approaching you in the approved way and that is OK?

Would that work for you?

Well, by and large it hasn't. Of course, if you do announce, in a conventional religion, that you have been talking with God and God has been talking with you, you are likely to get slung out.

Not always, some are relatively authentic. Still, this seems to suit your right now.

And another thing: it seems to me, that conventional religions don't teach you how to pray.

You are speaking from experience of certain Christian churches.

OK, that's what I mean by conventional religion.

17

And how would you teach people how to pray?

Well, I haven't mastered it yet, but here are some observations and I hope to discover some new points for myself. Begin by getting still, or at least as still as you can. Focusing on your breath for a few minutes is a great way to do this. It's much easier than trying to think of nothing, which in my experience creates a vacuum that continues to attract things, ideas, words, into. So go with the breath.

Having done this for a while, just notice if there if there is something there to focus on; it's the equivalent of looking in your prayer box. Just see if there is something important there for you. Let's say there is nothing in particular there right now; that's OK.

You might put some gentle intent out into the space in front of you. If you don't have anything in particular, a great line is "Thy will be done", which almost everyone knows.

Why is it a great line?

Because you don't have to make any thing up, you don't have to rely on your own flawed perspectives, you don't have to have pre-pared intent to go into prayer, you can just turn up. Another thing about "Thy will be done" is that it presupposes you are surrendering to the divine, which turns out to be a very liberating thing to do; not having it our own way makes us free, whereas having to have it our own way makes us in chain to our will, but I digress. And it can be helpful to say "Thy will be done" a number of times.

You are making progress.

During the "Thy will be done" you might get a sense of something, perhaps a sense of being protected of being cosseted, and that's great if you pick up that.

During this time it's good to focus on our breathing. It seems to help to keep balance. During this prayer time, I don't usually ask for or get anything specific, and I am not sure what to ask for. The point is "Thy will be done", so I can't push for anything.

But there is something I sometimes do, that I feel is completely

OK. I send light to people.

Please explain.

I picture someone, typically I start with individual members of the family, and then I see them bathed in bright, white light. It's like I am sending light out of my outbox to them. This feels great to me and I would like to do it more often. What's your perspective?

Whatever gets you through the light.

I light that!

Me too: How does your work differ from the common form of prayer?

Well, prayer is supposed to be hard, but this form of prayer is easy. In prayer you are supposed to come up with a series of requests, which means you have to do a fair amount of preparation, making it harder still, but this way no preparation is necessary. Here's the key thing: in this form you aren't using your willpower in any shape or form. And that feels great to me. But isn't there a problem?

Namely.

Don't we need to know your will?

Do you? Can you learn to trust me?

Yes, I can. I think I am. But don't we sometimes need to know your will in order to do your will?

Could you settle for a sense of being guided?

OK, I agree. The sense of being guided is there for any of us all of the time, including me. how does that work?

How do you experience it?

I think it has something to do with an openness on my part. Conversely, when I am not experiencing it, it has something to do with a closedness on my part. So I have to start with being open and still. And then it is just there, as if by magic, it's there without a thought, it's there before a thought, without fanfare. That moment has been perfect: the words have been spoken, the book has been lifted off the shelf.

The experience of the sense of being guided seems to apply to the short-term, to this moment, it never seems to be about the medium or long term, there are no goals or objectives, they seem to be up to me.

They are.

OK. So I get to set my goals.

You do. That's what you do.

So then I am pursuing my will.

Which is my will.

3. Energy and Death

It has always seemed to me like a great mystery, but a mystery which may be explicable. Here we are conscious beings in the world, with no apparent memory of anything before this life, and so no basis for believing that we somehow created ourselves, so we are the created, and yet we do not, apparently, know the creator.

Defying the basic laws of physics, we are, it would seem, an uncaused consequence, we are human beings without a cause. Yet this makes no sense. Alternatively we created ourselves or we were created by a creator.

Or both.

How do you mean, both?

You are created by a creator and you created yourself.

How on earth can both be true?

Not on earth. At the micro level, you created this life. You drew it towards yourself and you are still doing this. At the macro level, you and the creator are one.

How can that be?

Did you think there was one creator or more than one creator?

Only one: but who creates the creator?

The creator is the uncaused cause.

But how can that be?

How can that not be? How can you not have an uncaused cause?

The Big Bang.

And who or what caused that?

The Big Collapse.

As it was, and it is, and it shall forever be. In the beginning was the uncaused cause.

I have another question. I have read there are millions of stars in the Milky Way and there are millions of Milky Ways in the universe. That's quite an undertaking. Why bother?

It was no bother. It was just a thought.

How does that work?

Whatever I think is. As the creator, you could say I dreamt the whole thing up.

Whatever happened to free will?

You get to dream things up too.

So now, which of us is doing the dreaming?

There is no part of you that is not part of me.

So we are co-creating.

Yes we are.

But for us, creating is a little bit harder.

You make it seem that way.

Really?

Creating is easy. You are doing it all the time.

How do we do it?

You are thinking, feeling, energising.

And that is how we create? It doesn't feel like a complete description.

Language doesn't work too well here. Let's use another word, and then pin its meaning down more precisely. The word is intend.

The future awaits your intentions!

Yes, of course.

Or as Einstein put it, "Your imagination is your preview of life's forthcoming attractions". Tell me more about how intent works.

You already know.

OK, focus is important. You can't focus on everything. You have to be selective. Then the direction of thought has to be right. You can be focusing on what you do intend or you can think you are focusing on what you do intend while actively focusing on what you do not intend. This has been beautifully spelt out in *"Ask and it is given"*, for which many thanks. Then the energy has to be right.

Explain.

Your energy has to be in the right place. Actually, your energy has to be consistent with what you are focusing upon. You have to be there with your energy to be a creator.

And where is your energy most of the time?

Oh, it's floating around where I am, going nowhere in particular.

And that's how you keep things the way they are, which is not such a bad thing.

But it is not so great.

Not when you want to create something different. Be there first.

What?

Be in the space of that which you want to create. Be the space creator.

Well that sounds fun.

It is.

I am just absorbing that.

And having absorbed it …

I can be more aware of what I am creating more of the time. I can be more aware of my energy and more selective in what I focus upon. But there's a hard part.

Namely.

In my experience, there are lots of disturbing elements. I have tried to cut most of them out, or at least severely reduce them – newspapers with screaming headlines and TV and radio news with all of its negativity – but there is still negativity around.

And people wonder why you cut out so much media.

Because it doesn't help, that's the real reason. It doesn't make a positive difference. It just reflects a broken world.

Is "broken" a bit strong?

Well it's fragmented, it's cut off, it's even desperate. Behind that, within that, is an amazing beauty. When you are confronted with let us say foolishness, it is important to sense the wonderful being hidden within.

And how do you do that?

It's always there. With practice it is difficult not to sense it. In India and Nepal there is a powerful practice of greeting another person by pressing hands together as though in prayer, saying Namaste, and offering a little bow, which means something like, "I salute the divine within you". Can I bring in that Hello is a shortening of "Be thou whole" and Goodbye is a shortening of "God be with you".

I am. There is no other way. I cannot not be that which I have created.

And what we've created?

We are one.

So where were we?

We were creating and we still are.

We seem to be darting around a bit. One subject gives rise to another, and so on.

Where would you like to go next?

I still haven't quite covered the business of external disturbances creeping in.

> They are internal.

Meaning?

> They are already within you.

So how do I see them off, how do I get rid of them?

> You can transmute them. Intend every external disturbance is transformed as it comes into your energy field into something that makes you feel really calm.

That feels good. I could imagine it soothing my solar plexus. That was great, I just heard some discordant voices on the other side of the street outside the window where two young adults were cursing while lighting up, their voices heavy with negative energy and I just imagined myself receiving something cool and calm, a beautiful balm.

> Good and what else could you have done?

I could have sent some of that calming energy back to them. And with the next passing couple – a couple of moments have passed – I have.

> You know how to do this stuff. Why do you do so little of it?

Wow, imagine I could do that all the time.

> You can, it is what you are there for.

So the rest of the time is a waste of time?

> You have to prepare and you choose to share.

I have said that I want to be a great spiritual teacher. It's not exactly a wannabee, it's a feeling of a calling.

> I am calling you and you are calling me.

The great bit, isn't, I hope, to make me feel important but because there is no point being a not-too-great spiritual teacher. It's important.

> And what would be more important than feeling important?

Feeling loved.

And do you?

Yes, I do. But I see there is something more. I had thought I could provide a useful service simply by understanding the great spiritual works and simplifying them so they are more accessible to more people. But now I am beginning to realise I have to be pretty good spiritual practitioner too.

How could it be otherwise? There is practice and there is non-practice and that's it.

Life could be like a long, religious poem, walking in sunlight.

Becoming sunlight.

How do you mean?

You are all the sons and daughters of the light. Let the light flow through you, and let your light shine. How does that feel?

It feels brilliant, thank you.

Tell me about death.

There is no death; just a big once in a lifetime change. Let's call it the big change.

OK, tell me about the big change.

It's worth getting ready for.

And how do I do that?

Well, you are going to lose everything. So you might like to relax your hold upon them, so it won't feel like they are yanked away from you. It would help if you would get over this whole idea of ownership.

Ownership is wrong?

It is a self-limiting illusion. Instead of ownership, think in terms of stewardship. The whole thing is on loan.

Do we have to pay interest?

As a steward, you have an opportunity to be creative. You don't even own your body.

I don't?

You are constantly borrowing cells, for example from the food you eat, and then you are giving them back. Generally you get to borrow material for up to two years.

Then I have to give it back.

You always do give it back.

What about my family?

It is not yours singular, it would be better to say it is yours plural, but even this places a tighter limitation that you may now find useful. You are part of the one; that is all.

At the time of the big change you move from one part of the one to another part of the one. Trying to hold onto things puts you in conflict with the process. Besides, as soon as you stewardship, the weight of everything drops from your shoulders, because it's not yours.

Stewardship does not mean that you won't live in a house and have proximity to others, you may well do. You may buy things and the legal system may regard you as the owner, but you are merely the steward, and this is freedom.

When you won you aren't free?

When you have a feeling of ownership towards something, that is a limiting feeling. When you feel you have a right to something that others don't have, that is limiting.

I thought we were talking about the big life change?

Well, this is the big life change. It will help you get ready for the upcoming big life change.

You are.

4. The Time-Box

OK, I am here again.

Hear again.

But unsure what we should focus on, and unsure if I will hear you well. I have a nervousness, an apprehension at the start of a session, but when I reflect I realise that it must be entirely down to me, you are always there, always listening, always responding.

Here.

So I don't need to worry about you.

You don't need to worry about anything.

So why do I?

You worry that you will fall when you become imbalanced. When you are balanced, you don't fall.

Balance, that's all?

And presence: be here now.

Right, when I am worrying I am thinking about things that haven't happened and may never do so, which is made when I think about it. And focusing on what I don't want to happen won't help what I do want to happen to happen. So I should be present.

When you are focused on the present you don't worry.

But isn't it sometimes useful to focus on the future.

What you give attention to expands. Think of attention as being like energy that energises whatever you give attention to. Attention is like sunlight; your attention is your sunlight.

OK, let's come back to the present. How do I get back into the present, for example when I notice I am worrying?

Stop. Breathe, breathe slowly, breathe deeply, make physical contact with the world that is presently around you; touch a wall, stroke a carpet, feel the texture. Notice the present. You can't stop anything by trying to stop doing it, because you are just giving

28

more attention to it. Instead, focus on something else. In this case you are shifting your awareness from internally imagined worries to external reality. The present moment is a great place to be.

Because?

In the present moment everything is perfect. Actually, in the present moment nothing is happening.

Really?

In the present moment there is only the bliss of being. Events have happened or maybe about to happen. Either way, they aren't happening now.

This doesn't quite make sense.

Think of it as being like a movie. If you pause the tape, what is happening?

Nothing, it's just freeze frame. But in real life, things are always happening, you can't just stop the tape.

Actually, you can. Have you ever had the experience of time flying by?

Yes.

Or of time really dragging?

Of course.

What do you suppose is happening?

I don't know.

Suppose you could slow it down to a stop.

How would that work?

When time flew for you did it fly for everyone else in the world?

Unlikely.

When time stops for you need it stop for everyone?

It need not.

You could slip into the bliss of the present anytime. When you do so, you are stepping outside the constraints of time.

Has everyone ever done this?

Sure, everyone does this.

When?

When you leave the world, when you make the big change we were talking about, time stops.

But not for everyone else.

Correct. You just step out of the time box. You're somewhere else, you're somewhen else.

Am I someone else?

You are yourself. Right now, you are a fragment of yourself: the fragmentary self.

This makes sense to me. It feels as though a part of me is missing. There's an unsensed space. And it's much more obvious in present moment awareness. So time is just a construct?

Isn't everything a construct?

Yes, everything has been created.

So has time, and it doesn't work the way you think.

I've often wondered about how time, described as the fourth dimension, really works. When you move from one room to another, you don't suppose the previous room ceases to exist. You imagine it is still there. But when you move from one moment to another, we suppose the previous moment no longer exists, but it does, doesn't it?

What do you sense?

I sense that within the time box things happen sequentially, viewed from outside the time box, it is happening all the time. From outside the box, you could see the whole thing. But what about the future? That would mean the future could be seen too.

It's not the future.

It isn't?

When you are outside the time box.

But doesn't this mean everything that is going to happen is going to happen?

Everything that is going to happen is going to happen.

And doesn't that mean that we don't have free will?

No, you have free will: the fact that you will choose what you will choose does that mean that you will not make a choice. You are constantly making choices. You are choice-makers.

But you can step outside the box.

Of course, I can, I am outside the time box.

So you can see what will be.

Yes, all of it. How can I not see all of it?

So you are an all-knowing God, which means that nothing ever surprises you, because you already know it. And nothing we do ever disappoints you.

But you can disappoint yourself. Within the time box you don't see everything, so you do have surprises and disappointments. It keeps it interesting.

But, presumably, less interesting for you, as you already know all the outcomes.

Actually, it stays very interesting for me, because I get to experience what you experience.

Really?

All of it, how can I not?

That would amount to a lot of experiencing.

It does.

I wondered whether the only reason this moment exists is so you can experience it. For if it did not exist you would not experience it. And if you imagine it, it exists, for what God imagines, is.

Through creation, I experience vulnerability.

But you are invulnerable.

And through your – apparent – vulnerability I get to experience that feeling.

You say our "apparent" vulnerability. Are we invulnerable?

How do you experience yourself to be?

I sense I am absolutely and completely and divinely protected at all times and in all places. And I would maintain this view even if I were to be struck down by lightning.

Even if that brought this life to an end.

Especially so. At that point I am absolutely, completely divinely protected at all times and in all places even though there may no longer be any time or places. Actually, that would make life a lot easier.

Because ...

Without a body life is much simpler.

Actually, you may experience time and place.

I thought you said I would be out of it.

You will be out of the time box and you will be in another one.

Wow, no escape.

What's wrong with time? It's essential to all relative experience. You cannot have the things that make your life what it is, without time. Why would you want to escape?

I don't, and it's fine here. Incidentally, I'll be very happy not to have a lighting attack in the near future, or any time.

Why Is that?

Well, I enjoy it here. I also have a sense of incompleteness in another respect, that there is stuff to do here that I haven't done. A feeling that if I return without dong that which I came to do, this life would not have been what it was supposed to have been.

By who?

By me, by my greater self. I mean the whole me, the holy me, not the current fragment I experience being.

And you said return.

Yes, it must be a return. As much as any spatial word can make sense here. When I am reunited with my greater self, I am home, wherever that may be.

Home is where the soul is.

But I don't have to wait until this life is over to be in touch with my soul. So I can be at home in the here and now.

Yes you can.

Still, I think the experience following the end of this life will be very familiar to me.

And why might that be?

Because I have been there before. And I have done that before. I have stepped out of this life into that other life, which also means I have been into this world more than once.

Really.

It makes perfect sense to me this way. It feels completely right to me this way. You are unlimited. It is in your nature to do things in a big way. In a single life we get to experience a range of things, but it is short of complete. My experience of my kids is they already bring a lot of character, strengths and dispositions into the world that were pre-formed. We develop in some ways, but few of us become the finished article in a particular life. I think it will take me many lives to become the finished article.

The finished article: what is that?

I realise I don't know. How's about the most perfect expression of you? But that doesn't feel right as most is a comparative word, and if something is a perfect expression of you, that will do. Most is superlative. I'm a little lost, can you help me here?

You are expressing yourself.

And?

In doing so you express me.

So I can go on expressing myself beyond this life?

What do you think?

I will?

What do you intend?

I will.

5. Creation and Attachment

OK, I am here again and I'm excited, though I am not sure whether I should have an agenda or be agenda-free.

Listen to me.

OK, I am ready and listening, but how well? I need to get still.

Why do you worry I won't be here for you?

I know you will be here. It's just a matter of me tuning in. I am still grappling with the business of your will and my will. If I want thy will to be done and your will is that our will be done, how do we get started?

Listen to me, it's a partnership. We are interchanging ideas all the time. So what is your will? (I'm listening.)

OK, right now, it is that this be a highly practical and inspirational work that allows millions of human beings to move forward in their lives.

Except they are not human beings. Most of the time – leaving the human bit for a moment – they are human thinkings, human talkings and human doings.

And the human bit?

We aren't human, human means of the ground, we are divine.

OK, we are divine beings who act as though we are human processors. So how do we make the shift?

Detach from the process, align with the divine.

There's a lovely little exercise that helped me to get the idea of detaching. You look at your hand and ask yourself are you your hand or the one who observes your hand. You notice a thought and you ask yourself are you your thought or the one who observes the thought, and so on. Non-attachment comes through sensing you are none of the things you sense, observe, see, not even your thoughts, emotions, or body.

You are the still small voice within.

I don't see myself as the one who changes, not even as the one who ages. I am unchanging.

You experience change.

I am the unchanging one who experiences change.

Just like me.

Why is it important to detach?

When you detach you are at peace.

Right, when you are attached to a turbulent world your life will be turbulent.

When you detach you are free.

Imperturbable would be free.

When you detach you are invulnerable.

Aren't you invulnerable anyway?

Yes, but the you who you have identified with isn't invulnerable. In fact, that you is certain to be destroyed.

Can you detach and yet live in the world with your thoughts, emotions and physical body?

Yes, non-attachment is an attitude, a feeling, a way. When you are non-attached, you don't stop having thoughts, emotions, or anything else, you don't disconnect from your body.

I can also be non-attached to results, can't I? Would you explain how you can be non-attached to results and still have clear intent?

It's simple. Non-attachment works in the present. Intent reaches out into the future.

So you can have intent without attachment?

Intent is creation, attachment is consumption.

To be a creator you must intend, while to be divine you must be unattached. But why intend something if you don't want to attach to it?

You can intend to have more love in your life without being attached to it. In fact, attachment stifles creation, it blocks the flow.

Right, when you have a fair degree of intent out there and the process of creation is under way, and your attachment leads you to conclude that it's not there, because it is not yet there you 'untend'.

Yes, human beings spend a lot of their time untending.

We notice it is like this. We say we would like it to be like that, but we say it will never be like that because it is like this. Perfect untent.

The biggest obstacle to creation of the new is attachment to the old. However, it is set up so change is unavoidable; death and birth are constantly present.

Without your kind of dramatic change we might settle for keeping things the same. But a life of repetition without any new ingredients would be a different kind of death. There is always the prospect of growth and there is always the prospect of death. Each feeds the other.

And neither is real.

Growth can be experienced.

Yes, it is a convincing illusion. But you are growing into yourself.

And everything already exists. However, within the time-box everything is unfolding.

And as a flower unfolds, the lotus is already within.

This whole dialogue feels unintentional.

But at another level you have summoned it up. Intent is operating perfectly.

I'm still pretty good at being untentional, most of the time really. If I could just get out of the way and of my intent, everything would flow.

Perfect intent feels fairly unintentional. A little intent goes a long way.

I have to stop contaminating intent with untent. It feels like I have been doing it to myself. It has often felt that way when I have been into self-blame, but this time it seems clearer. And I don't feel like blaming anyone, it's just that I've been practicing for what feels like a very long time.

What else is there to do?

6. Sitting in Silence

It's been a while but I am back. I'm clearer on this. It's absolutely not a matter of whether you are around. You always are. You cannot not be: the only question is attunement. And thank you, for the continuing spiritual encouragements along the way. All I really have to do is take one step in your direction – open my eyes just a little more – and I am encouraged.

Would you like to explain?

Well, I have spent the vast majority of my life distracted, focused on the affairs of the world, but I have only to incline my attention towards you, only to ask for your guidance and being me feels different. I am likely to feel calmer and clearer, and the problem is likely to seem less pressing.

Anyone can do this.

Yes, anyone can do this anytime, but there seem to be more effective ways to do so. It's better to be calm, it helps to take deep breaths, it's good to be present, by which I mean let go of the not-here and the not-now. Be as unencumbered as you possibly can.

OK, it's your call.

And as you know, I get more specific spiritual encouragements, and they are just wonderful. And I am completely convinced they are available to us all.

So be it.

So why don't many others get them?

They do, in their way. They get what they can.

But they could get so much more.

And so could you, couldn't you?

Yes I could.

And why don't you?

I'm busy, I'm tired, and when I am neither of them, most often I

39

find something else to focus on.

> Why is that?

The world is interesting, absorbing, enjoyable, the process of being here is quite diverting.

> So that's OK.

It doesn't feel quite enough: To come into the world, be here for a while, and then leave, without having understood the before and after, the world outside the world.

> The world inside the world.

OK, the Kingdom of heaven is within.

> It is written.

I am not sure where this conversation is leading.

> Because ...

I am not sure of my intent in being here.

> We could sit in silence.

OK, let's do that.

7. The Creator is No Thing

OK, I am here.

And I am here.

Thank you for this, thank you for everything. The created thanks the creator, from which we come.

You are never really separate.

Though it often seems like that. I just turned to a bookshelf and my eyes lighted on a "One", the title of a Richard Bach book, thanks again.

Separation is not without promise, the promise of unification. In fact, without separation, there is no promise. It shall be.

It was, it is, it shall be.

Amen.

Thank you for the promise and thank you for the separation.

In knowing ourselves separately, we know different aspects of ourselves.

Which helps us to experience ourselves more completely.

Though nothing is ever complete. Existence could only complete itself in non-existence.

I understand incompletely.

Did you ever think you could talk to God?

I – almost always when I thought about it – felt there had to be something.

I am no thing.

OK, I felt that for the created to exist there had to be a creator.

Nothing comes from nothing.

Yes, the created could not create - for the first time - the created, because the created did not exist. However much you break down the development of life into minutes, steps, you are still left with this.

Nothing could not create something?

But actually that's the only way, no thing created something.

Which is essentially what I did. And actually I continue to do it, it is happening all the time. Existence is blinking into and out of existence all the time, your scientists are beginning to discover this. It is pulsing.

So you are nothing.

I already said that I am nothing.

I like to call you the creative force.

That's a useful term. You are creative when you work with the creative force. Actually you set the tempo.

I want to continue.

With?

With this conversation, with this moment, with the next moment, with relationships, with discovery, with life: with everything and with nothing. There's a problem about leading and following. I want to follow you.

Be a leader in following me.

Why should anyone follow you?

You already know this.

Because when I follow you I am complete. It's a radically different way of being. Everything just flows, more than that, everything is alight. More than that, everything is light.

Complete.

I'm encountering space again. A place of choices, or of potential choices, but more have sprung to mind.

Space is OK.

I love the idea you are right here. I don't think I need you to say anything. Just feeling some presence is enough. I love the feeling of the breeze on my hands and face. OK now where was I?

Where were you?

I was separate and now if feel conjoined, joined at the hip, like a Siamese God; cosseted, loved. I wonder if it might be appropriate to explore the question of how most people can experience more of your presence.

Why is this important to you?

Because there is a sense in which they are me and I am them, we are all one. So I wish this for them.

You have wishes for them.

Yes, I wish them light, love and latitude. Light is everything, it is in everything, so on reflection I wish the awareness of the light, actually to see the light! Love is source, love is in all, love is all, and latitude as we all need a lot of latitude, it conveys the idea of sideways movement, which I like. Latitude is, I suppose, a synonym for forgiveness. Light, love and latitude. I light it!

So what is your wish for them?

To lighten up.

And how can they do that?

In many ways, they can slow down, take it easy, enjoy the world. They can make time for each other, they can make time for themselves, they can breathe easier, they can look after their minds, they can look after their energy. But this is facilitated by sensing who they are, or first by sensing who they are not.

It's time to explain.

People seem to be really confused about who they are. They confuse themselves with their possessions, for example, they say "I am rich", but this immediately creates a problem, it introduces a fear of loss of self, because one day they won't be rich, and they deeply know this. The same point applies to status, intelligence, looks. People say "I am an architect", "I am clever" or they wonder if they look good.

What do you propose?

Let's completely give up on the idea of owning things and replace ownership with stewardship. You know, we probably think we own the earth! Stewardship is much more practical. Professionally, I propose we give up on being this or being that and replace it with, I have a responsibility for short. The ideas of stewardship and responsibility aren't meant to weigh us down, but to free us up. In this context, they help to avoid sublimating our identity in time-bound concepts.

I'd like to go further and give up on the idea of "my". "My" introduces the idea of attachment to something, and in almost all cases "My house, my friends, my body" it introduces the idea of attachment to something that won't be around long, so it presupposes the idea of loss. "My" also introduces the idea of separateness. If it's mine it's not yours, and that doesn't feel right. My anything limits my freedom!

And what difference will all of this make?

We'll come to know who we really are. Divine sparks cloaked in matter. Along the way the world gets kinder. Once we sense we are all of the same kind, kindness expands. Once we stop trying to take from one another, as there is no other, taking ceases.

So we are all one.

Yes, but there is a problem with my logic. I've suggested you can get to know who you really are when you realise who you are not. But people whose identity springs from money, status and power are reluctant to give them up, and about as reluctant to realise that's not them. Without an awareness of the spiritual, it's hard to give up on the material. You would be reluctant to give up on who you are not if you don't know who you are. Why give yourself up for what may appear to be nothing?

No thing.

8. A Little Light Working

Thank you for this day and this time. It's amazing to have this closeness and this freedom. And I wonder if we might start this session with decision-making. If I want thy will to be done then how do I know what to do?

You know this stuff. You listen. And you do what feels light.

What feels light; not right.

You know what is right for you when you feel what is light.

How do I do that?

You compare the lightness of anything with the lightness of anything else.

But you have just told us how to divine what is light for us. What do you want us to do?

I don't have wants or needs for that matter. How could I? I am already complete. If I wanted something it would exists in the same instant as I "wanted" it, figuratively speaking, but in as much as you want the right path, choose the light path.

You are familiar with the idea of things flowing, like water, and you know that's more elegant, than solid matter. Light is ultra-flow. It's as flowing as it gets.

How could I get more light into my life?

Walk in the light, call upon the light, work with your light. You think I am talking figuratively, I am talking literally. There is more light in and around you than you have imagined, let alone seen. You have started to do this.

Yes, I call down light and imagine it flowing through and around my body. I can't say I am sure what I am doing, and don't know the full significance is of this, but it feels good, and it seems to change me, to take me to a gentle place, it's quite extraordinary. So I'm, working with it, but there's much more to come, isn't there? I've hardly begun.

Everything has a beginning.

OK, it's up to me if I want to say more, there is a light energy around everything. It's see-through and yet it is clearly visible.

Everything has light.

I hesitate to say more.

You don't want to enlighten?

I don't want to put myself in a place where people say, "He is different to us".

Because you are not.

Anyway, how should I work with this energy-light?

Work is the light. Work in the awareness of the light. Let your light shine.

9. Show me the Way

Show me the way.

Walk with me and I will show you the way. You have heard that before. Now, are you willing to do it?

Yes, but explain to me, and aren't you always by my side?

You aren't always conscious of my presence.

So when I am not aware of your presence you don't show me the way?

You are much less receptive. And your action is less loving.

So you show me the way, as it were, one step at a time.

I show you your next step, depending on where you are.

You don't show me the whole thing, the whole way that I have asked to be shown.

Would you want to see the whole thing?

Well, I suppose it would take the fun out of it, I mean if I could see all of the steps of this life laid out in front of me, it might make living them all out a little duller.

And you crave excitement.

Yes, I do. Why do I?

Because you are not entirely comfortable with who you are.

Because I sense I am so much more than I appear to be.

And you are.

So my preference is for you to show me the way, step by step.

And

To walk with you

Which means …

To walk in awareness of you. And then how do I get it?

47

You are getting it. Little by little

But not when I become fearful.

Fearfulness is a good indicator that you have forgotten me.

So I should remember that all is well. Some people think that's a pretty silly idea, at odds with reality.

Wouldn't you rather be at odds with reality?

Yes, I like being at odds with reality, I like resisting stupidity and thoughtlessness and deceit. But now I am confused. I thought we had to accept the present moment, go with the flow.

Let's start with all is well, it's important you remember that all is well and you live in the wellness. It is and you are, whatever happens in this world, this remains true.

But it's not many people's experience, and so, even though all may really be well, if they don't experience it that way, it might as well not be,

It might as well be, you are a transformational being. You transform the environment around you. To make a sick world better, you must already be in wellness, whatever is happening on the surface, you have to connect with all-is-wellness at a deeper level.

Especially when things don't appear well.

It's all a matter of vibration, to transform something you have to give it a different vibration. This is obvious in some cases. Someone's anger could upset you, alternatively if, when they are angry, you remain calm, they will feel that, and that will affect them: transformation.

The way is transformation. I have this enduring feeling that I am great.

You are.

But I don't really seem to be delivering great work.

You have time.

I am like a butterfly that hasn't taken flight, or if there was any flight it was momentary. If I have understood you correctly, transformation or becoming is the key. And the key to outer transformation is inner transformation. We radiate what we are. To have something, we have to become energetically aligned with it. Energy isn't thought, but different thoughts, whether auditory, visual, or of a different form, generate different energies, and it is these that are influential. Thoughts create feelings about the thoughts that stimulate energies that pull the manifestation of the thought towards us or push it away or move it sideways or leave it where it is.

Is that what you think or is that what you feel?

The thoughts feel clear to me,. I think it is about clarity. The clearer we are the better. The clearer we are the clearer the result. What will you say?

If you have faith the size of a mustard seed you can move mountains.

Faith is knowing?

You know, you are practicing. You are all waking up to who you are. You are realising your potential for realising your potential.

10. Wanting

What do you want?

I want to be closer to you.

You are.

All the time

And ...

I want to have earned lots of cash.

Because

I will be clearer that I have been successful and I won't have to worry about bills and I will be free to do what I want to do.

You are free, you don't have to worry and you are successful. What if you could know you are successful in another way, without receiving cash, just form positive feedback from others? What if you know you would always be able to pay bills for I would always look after you? And what if you realise you are free to do what you want to do in this moment and in all moments?

Then I wouldn't need to have made lots of money. Is my feeling that I need to have earned lots of money simply a measure of my lack of trust in you.

And in you.

Am I that insecure?

Tell me, what do you want?

To have lived a life of which I am proud. A life of joy and love and significant giving. A life of stepping into the light, a life lived in the light. A life that takes a big step towards transcendence.

Then so be it. You always get what you choose. You are made in my image. You are constantly in the business of creating reality. Mostly, you are photocopying reality: each day is like the preceding day. You could be so much more creative.

How can we do that?

Detach. Let it be. Let it go. Don't be invested in how it is or isn't, don't react and don't let the world drag you down. You can only give yourself. Raise yourself and you raise the world.

This feels to me like hard work.

Developing any capability takes practice. And you have all the time in the world.

I keep being diverted.

Be yourself.

Even when diverted?

Always and in all places let your light shine.

And when I encounter the darkness?

Let your light shine. Could it be any simpler?

11. Asking

Here I am back in Istanbul. Thankful, relaxed and perhaps ready for another conversation.

Perhaps.

OK, I wish to say I am ready, I want it to be the case that I am ready, but I don't feel sure.

Do you have to have the answer?

Do I have to have the question … Can I start anywhere?

You are starting here.

It has felt like I have to have the answer to all of life's most profound questions. But we could just go one instant at a time, allowing everything to unfold at its own pace.

You could set the pace.

How do I do that?

You have to lift yourself up.

One step at a time.

One breath at a time.

"We lift up our hearts"

Do you?

Now and again. I want your help in doing this more and more. I ask you to bless each breath along the path.

I ask you to ask.

I just have.

Again and again.

I can't ask just once.

You can. But you keep on asking for different things.

Can I put the blessed breath at the top of my list?

You are sure there's nothing higher?

Can I get back to you on that? I'll let you know if I change my mind.

You do. Constantly.

OK, I wish to be led by you every step of the way.

Except when you don't – when you want to make your choices.

I do this?

Every step of the way. For example you ask your stomach what it would like to eat. You don't ask me.

That's trivial.

I could go on about how you go on with your choices, are you getting this?

Yes, I think so: God consciousness extends to the little things.

Every moment of every day, if that is your wish. And what difference will that make to you?

Blessed, beautiful, flowing, almost unconsciousness: I become like a bystander. Loving yet disinterested: Magical too, and transformatory for me and others. Am I getting closer?

As close as you want.

OK, I feel I am on the path.

You are, always.

You make this sound so easy.

That's because it is. Easier, for example, than the alternative.

So whenever I lose consciousness of you – as I did a few moments ago, after reflecting on always – I should just bring it back to you?

As you wish

And this won't make my life duller?

It will make it fuller.

Something interesting happened in the Grand Bazaar today. I was looking for an Aladdin's lamp and try as I might, none came into sight. I asked that you would take over the walk. A few minutes later if stopped at a stall and found myself staring at some goods and not seeing any of them. Then I noticed they were Aladdin's lamps. Thanks for that, it is brilliant that you will even direct my eyes.

I am as wiling as you are.

I thought your will was unstoppable.

That's why I constrain it, to match yours. It is as I choose, and I choose to be as willing as you are.

OK, what is your will for the human race?

It is evolving.

What is your will?

It is reaching upwards. As it will.

And your will is different?

My will is the same. We are in this together.

It feels like we are in this and you are out of this.

Except when you invite me in. but really I am there anyway.

But really, are we evolving upward? It seems like there is more war, more conflict, more want than ever before.

You amplify it, you broadcast it, you spread it around, you depress yourselves. You are pretty good at that.

Yes, more of us are depressed these days.

Why not be uppressed? Fill your lives with things that uppress you instead of things that depress you.

Will that make the depressing things go away?

It will localize them.

Won't that mean we won't take appropriate action?

You don't anyway. And when you are confronted with darkness what is appropriate action?

Brighten the light.

So why not do that anyway?

12. Time and again

OK, I am here again, here again meaning attentive. And it feels as though the world makes perfect sense. I am looking at a bush while sitting on a rooftop balcony and the wind plays gently on my face, hands, and ankles. It's a good place to be.

Where else would you rather be?

Nowhere else, it is perfect. Equally, anywhere else with sunlight and breeze, and with or without distant noises of the world, a ship's horn, a passing train, it makes no difference. Stillness is carried inside you. So I am very thankful.

For what?

The gift of being: we the created, thank you, the creator; we who did not create ourselves and who did not create this moment.

But you did create yourselves as you are and you did create this moment.

How?

You called it forth.

And we called forth ourselves.

You called forth the way you are.

How did we do this?

You live lives of modest expectation and you fulfil your expectations. You ask me for almost nothing, turning to me most often when you are desperate. By and large, you are creating yourselves, within the timebox.

And that doesn't disappoint you?

Nothing disappoints me. It's the way you make it.

Made in your image, as creators we are. And how are we doing?

Uneven progress.

And how do we make more even progress?

Change yourselves from the inside out. Here's an easy way to do this. Focus on the perfection in every place, in every moment in everything.

The world seems far from perfect.

The perfection is not being seen. That bush is perfect, a snowflake is perfect. The air is perfect, your heart is perfect, the sun is perfect, perfection is all around you. Do you not see it? Perfection is inside you too. You are perfect too. This is the perfect moment. All moments have conspired to create this one, and we are creating more perfect moments: an infinity of instances. Do you see?

What difference does the realisation of perfection make?

It makes all the difference in the world. There is nothing more to get upset about – and no point in being upset – there is nothing to worry about – and no point in worrying – there is nothing to regret. It's all here now.

And no point in doing anything?

Every point to everything. It's always your point. That's the point, but something beautiful does happen when you realise the perfection in everything, you step outside of the timebox.

But I'm still here.

You have, as it were, one foot in and one foot out. You are aware of the bliss of the infinite.

Let me see if I have this. Perfection is experienced by becoming perfect. There is perfection all around us, but our own imperfections, our own obsession with the imperfect, prevent us from experiencing perfection, preventing us from becoming perfect.

Very neat, except that you are already perfect. You don't have any such becoming to do. Just experience it.

So, see it, hear it, feel it, taste it: the perfection of every moment. This doesn't seem too difficult.

See the perfection in others when they smile, see the perfection when they frown. See it when you encounter smoothness on your path, see it when you encounter a rock: it's a perfect rock. See the perfection in others all of the time and you may help them to see for they do not see it.

They have eyes but do not see.

Are you starting to see?

I think I am.

It's important not to beat yourself up about this, you've been doing imperfection very well. We might almost say you have been doing imperfection perfectly. Now it is time to do perfection perfectly.

So we don't need to change the world.

You don't need to do anything, but if you did want to change the world you would start by changing yourself. And then you would share yourself with the world. To make change, be the change. You cannot give what you do not have. And you have everything. How can human beings change if human beings like you do not change? As you stop being part of the problems, you start becoming part of the solution. You have said fear is the biggest problem in the world: can you see fear disappears as perfection is experienced? Judgement also disappears, wanting, needing, it all goes.

But we still get to make choices?

All the time, and the first choice is always: what's your focus? Everything proceeds from that. When you see the perfection in a thing, you are really seeing the life force, you are connecting at a much deeper level. And from here you resonate more powerfully.

When a part of creation sees the perfection in another part, it is no longer a part, it is whole, when a part is seen in this light, its perfection is affirmed, it is enlightened.

The sun has broken through the cloud as is glistening on the Sea of Marmara, it's a beautiful September afternoon.

See the perfection in everything and you nurture it, you nurture its awareness of its true nature.

This is what is meant by turning the other cheek?

When you encounter violence you are at a moment of choice. You can amplify the violence by joining forces with it, and in doing so you would validate the violator. Or you can strike a different note, you can communicate with the perfect being..

How do we do that?

See the perfection, feel the perfection. Align the two, and the perpetrator will be disarmed. Actually, as you practice perfection you will notice changes in your life. For example, you will notice that violations do not occur. Or if, occasionally, a potential violation intrudes you will be able to disarm it more or less instantly. Your presence will be enough.

That sounds awesome. I get the theory but feel a long way from it.

You say you will be a great spiritual teacher. Will you walk with me?

Yes I will.

It's time to walk the talk.

This isn't so easy. I was walking past a fenced garden of a house and a dog was barking and pushing on the fence, and I quietly commanded it to be still, and it wondered if it would stay quiet as I walked on, and it did. I wondered if it was co-incidence, if I just got lucky.

Also, it seems, the focus must not be on how I am doing, because then I am separate, I am seeing myself separately, and that would be enough to undo it, I have to be one with my focus.

Every moment, every place, every undulation has the opportunities – there cannot not be "opportunities" to be aware of your focus.

This makes "judge not" so clear, but judge not was a don't-do negative, and that's hard not to do. Seeing perfection is easier. I have long been attracted to the idea that "this is the best of all possible worlds" enunciated by Pangloss in Volatire's Candide, even though Voltaire lampoons it. When you see the perfection in each moment, it is as though this is the best of all possible worlds.

Ever present perfection.

So when it is raining, the problem isn't the rain, the difficulty lies in our reaction to it, when someone is threatening, the difficulty is in our reaction, when someone dies, the same applies. I have just about developed a sense that everything is always OK, come what may. My challenge is to realise how linked I am to everything else. When I do something well, I am likely to notice my contribution and feel special!

Your problem is not that you sometimes feel special: it is that you do not always know how special you are. If you knew how special you are you would have no need to demonstrate it, it is already so. Know that it is so and you are freed of the need to impress.

It is not the adequacy of theirs that creates tension, but their sense of their own inadequacy, which they feel they must countervail come what may.

Realise the perfection in yourself and in others and of course you realise that there is no other.

We are all the same?

You are all perfect. Live at that level of awareness and you appreciate unity. Are you getting it?

Sometimes I am experiencing the glory of being. Always I feel absolutely and divinely protected.

Now feel nurtured.

Yes, I get that.

The path is lit.

Then I must make tracks.

Tread lightly.

13. Perfection

I am here.

And what is your intent?

To continue co-creating a light upon the path; a source of wisdom and guidance; a series of blessings; and, as we do this to better know my way.

You have to become the way, you become truth, you become one with life, there is no other way.

The way, the truth and the life!

One with all of it, in the end, you cannot not become one with all of it.

There is no choice?

There is plenty of choice. You can go on deferring the end for as long as you choose. In the end, there is no separation. All roads lead ultimately to unity.

But you can move towards unity and away from it?

With each realization, it is very difficult to take a backward step, and it is hard to forget what you have come to know.

All roads lead to Rome, or in this case to Byzantium.

Rome is where your heart is.

So there is no failure.

There are set backs and spring forwards. But some of the greatest set-backs create the greatest spring forwards.

Can we talk about heaven here?

Heaven is in your heart. Heaven is a here and now thing, not a then and there thing, this is not a world to be endured pending arrival in heaven sometime, someplace, maybe. Enjoy heaven today.

Heaven is all around us?

Heaven is in your heart, let your love flow and you will be in heaven. As the heaven that is in you flows all around you, you will find that it is in you and you are in it. Unlock heaven.

I have given you heaven and the world.

We haven't known heaven is within our grasp.

It is not to be grasped; it is to be given away. You experience the kingdom of heaven by giving it away. It cannot be held.

You lose what you keep and you keep what you lose. If you want to be happier, cause others to be happy. If you want to experience love, love. If you want to experience the kingdom of heaven, give it away. This isn't our contemporary dogma.

It can be. It's the next step.

We spend most of our time working to gain money, power and status. Money and status are like drugs: there is never enough of them. And when we do have them, we are worried we will lose them. In so doing, we miss out on the kingdom of heaven.

This is unnecessary. Work doesn't have to be like that. You could value people equally, irrespective of their position. Is a good life a rich life?

Is a poor life a good life?

There is no connection between the two. Yet you strive for material wealth. Are you really passionate about money? Isn't it obvious: your material wealth wants are inexhaustible. Yet you don't really need to want anything. You could make your passion your work.

Your work could be a kingdom of heaven time, if you could make it so, you would, wouldn't you?

Yes.

Do so.

This isn't what I had in mind when I asked about heaven.

What did you have in mind?

Your Kingdom.

Is a here and now experience, I didn't send you out into the cold just so that you could one day return. You have gone there with everything you need for the journey, everything you need and more. Plus there are absolutely unlimited supplies to which you have access. You have only to ask ....

And it is given. But it rarely feels like that.

That's because you don't know how to ask.

How's that?

Ask as though you already have it.

Which isn't really asking, it is thanking: It's a kind of "thanking of making this so" even before it has been made so.

You do this with friends. After someone says they will do something for you, you may say, "Thanks for doing that". Treat me like a friend.

You highlight a first step – the friend agrees to do something – which supposes another step, that they are asked, so 1: ask, 2: agree, 3: thank.

Here's a preliminary step. You may want to consider carefully what you ask for. A lot of people make a lot of half-asked requests.

And you deny them?

They aren't sure what they want.

How can they get sure?

They can ask me.

When they don't know what to ask for, they can start the process by asking you?

Though there is a step before that. Before they ask they may want to have some kind of relationship with me.

You will deny them if they don't?

No, but they may not feel comfortable asking.

Having developed a relationship with you, and asked you what they should ask for, what's the next step?

Thank me for delivering it.

You want to be thanked?

It's absolutely unnecessary to me, but it does help people to accept the delivery. And I am only going to deliver for those who accept the delivery. In asking me for what they should have and in thanking me for its delivery the process is complete. By all means, you can confirm you do want what I offer you!

Why consult you? Why not just go after what we want? Aren't you supposed to go along with what we want?

You do and I do. That's most of what happens, but it's not very efficient because you are asking for things that won't get you what you want even when you get them. Checking your requests with me would save a lot of time.

It sounds like we haven't got it cracked.

Some of you don't ask. Others ask and cancel the order simultaneously. Intellectually you ask for it, emotionally you feel you can't have it. Others ask and feel you can have it, but it's not what you should have asked for in the first place.

How do we move forward from here?

Once our will is aligned we will do just fine.

I thought your will would follow our will.

Which is why I am inviting you to align your will with your will.

Excuse me?

Once your will is focused on where you really want to go, on where really works for you, bingo. There's another complication. You have to ask fairly consistently.

You don't take the order when it is given once?

Suppose someone asks that a particular meeting is really blessed and produces beautiful outcomes for all concerned. That's OK. But suppose subsequently, instead of imagining the meeting going that way, they worry about it going badly: they are now blocking the request.

And if someone momentarily wishes ill upon someone and then

thinks better of it, the ill doesn't get delivered either. That's a relief.

At your stage of evolution can you see it would be a disaster if I acted on all of your thoughts? It turns out most of your thoughts nullify most of the rest of your thoughts. For example, I want to be rich but am poor, I want to be thin but am overweight, I want to be loved but am unlovable, I want to be a great spiritual leader but am not.

Alright, you got me.

Beliefs aren't so easily changed. The mantra has power only when it is really believed.

So when Gandhi said, "Be the change you wish to see ...", he didn't just mean be an example to others, he also meant change is a matter of being.

The short-cut is being, did you think you weren't being, you are a being machine.

I'm a machine?

In the sense that you are constantly doing being: you are constantly creating, there is nothing else for you to do, so you cannot not create. There is no way for you to switch off the creation button. It's good to be aware you are constantly creating, better to be aware of what it is you are creating. It's even better to choose what you are creating, and it's best of all when we figure this out together.

14. The Distracted Age

I am here, fairly attentive, willing to be led.

And where would you like me to lead you?

Into greater understanding of the present.

Meaning

Understanding the gifts of life and of death.

I have told you: there is no death.

Then there is no escape from life.

Why would you want to escape from life?

To rest, one might like to rest.

As soon as you put down your burden, I pick it up.

"Come to me all you who are heavy burdened ..." now has a new meaning. Clarify intention and turn it over to you. When we make it our burden, we take it from you, we disempower God.

Empower God.

And there I was thinking you were all powerful.

I am. Within the Time-Box I allow you to choose your will, I empower you. How does it feel?

It feels increasingly powerful.

Now empower me. Hand the keys back to me. Allow me to do your will, choose the door through which you will walk, and let me do the rest.

And then I can rest. It sounds like I am making heavy weather of this. We are still dealing with intent.

And what do you intend?

So much of the time, I realise like mostly whenever you ask me, nothing much, just understanding, I have got past asking for your understanding, I think there is nothing you don't already understand, and I understand I am already forgiven, if there were any forgiveness to be given.

So what?

So we have an evolution of the human species, so we become more loving, more powerful and more sensitive, we experience more of the glory of life and we more beautifully reflect the glory of creation.

And how will you help to bring that about?

By going there myself, and by making it easier for others to go there too.

And what prevents you?

A lack of interest! We aren't really interested in building a better world and we aren't really interested in evolving our race.

Do you think you can?

Yes, but we don't even get as far as considering that question. We have misunderstood success. The development of the human race, the development of ourselves, even understanding why we are here, does not interest us. This is not a serious age. This is also not a joyful age.

The two could go together.

The serious has been displaced by the trivial. This is a trivial age. We spend our time like squirrels, marking out our territory, accumulating nuts, and eating them, and we rarely even jump from tree to tree. It's the distracted age: nuts, nuts, nuts.

And why is this?

Behind all this is fear, and behind the fear is disconnection from the source: you.

So what do you seek?

Reconnection, once you know that everything will always be provided, you stop struggling.

Then why do you struggle?

I'm still carrying my cares: pretty foolish really.

Lighten up.

15. Energy

I can't get over the idea that this is real. I mean the experience of being in the world at all, in fact even the experience of being anything. And then, on top of the actual experience of being, the awareness of the experience of being, that this is happening, feels magical; so far beyond any human conception as to be quite fantastic. Way beyond reason.

Which suggests limits to reason.

In this context of this fantastic awareness, the idea of a dialogue with you isn't so much more fantastic. Why shouldn't I accept this too? This feels a nice space in which to be. I am keen for it to continue now. The closer I feel to you the easier it is to sense appropriate direction. Everything is gentle, flowing, assured.

That is how it is meant to be.

The further I feel from you, the more I am lost: feeling more like a hunter who is being hunted.

It's a convincing illusion.

My hypothesis is: consciousness of you raises my vibration bringing me into a greater attunement.

It's the other way around. Raising your energy brings you greater consciousness,

How do I raise my energy?

Take time to be still and replenish, hydrate, breathe well, clarify.

This couldn't be simpler.

Let your busy thoughts go. Create some space for me.

This doesn't seem to involve any doing at all.

It's time to be.

For many years I have – occasionally – tried to be aware of you.

But this doing has slipped quickly into other forms of doing. When I've really tried, when things have seemed really tough, I have brought my emotional baggage along, and I haven't really got past that.

Don't try to be. All your trying takes you further away from being.

How can I do anything without trying?

Don't try, don't do, and definitely don't try to do. You know how to be: attune, ask and answer.

And to attune?

We've been talking about this. You can clarify your intent. You can ask for help with this.

Help me.

Become aware of your breath, slow it down. Imagine yourself climbing a stairway. Each floor represents a higher level of consciousness. At each level you can see more, you can feel more, you know more. Notice your consciousness changing.

OK, this works.

There are many ways. Discover what works for you.

One thing that works for me is observing myself: noticing the person I am apparently being. And then noticing I'm not the person I am noticing. Actually, I am the noticer.

You've noticed.

Such a simple exercise you can run again and again.

You can be aware.

And that's really the big difference.

It makes the big difference.

16. The Agenda

I am here, it's been a while, it has felt like a bit of a battle sometimes.

That's because you have been away.

Not all the time, I haven't been away all the time.

Come closer all the time.

I wish for nothing else.

You wish for lots of things, intermittently.

It feels to me that I am going round in circles.

Spirals, you are going round in spirals. Be still and know

That you are Lord?

Be still and know.

But I have so many things to do.

You are making them all up.

There will be consequences if I don't do them.

There are consequences when you don't get still. When you are still you are in the flow.

Now we have stillness and flow?

Everything is relative. Think of stillness as being like balanced. It's easier to go with the flow when you are balanced.

Like riding a bicycle. OK. It feels like I have to get the agenda here, it feels like you are listening, waiting,

So what's the agenda?

I don't know; it feels like I have many, I am not sure which way to turn.

The agenda is love, at all times and in all places, that's the agenda. OK?

Kind of, I feel pulled in different directions.

It is you who are pulling those directions towards you. And you know how.

It feels like I need to sort myself out. Would you help me with this?

That is what is happening here.

17. A Knowing Path

The path is clear when I am walking upon it, but when I am not walking it, it does not seem to be there. Even when I am on it, the next steps are not obvious, it is as though I am blind [or] extraordinarily short-sighted: the future, even near-term is a blur, I can only see the part of the path on which I am.

You are.

How do I know I'm on the path? Life is perfectly blessed, brimming with joy. The experience of living is joyful in the moment, and beautiful things happen, they come out of nowhere.

Not quite. You intend them.

In the moment, I experience boundless energy and freedom. There's a knowing, a presence and an absence of self.

I am here: there is nowhere else I would rather be.

This is learning about love, isn't it?

The world reveals itself to itself and I am revealed.

It feels like a very long time,

What's a lifetime in eternity?

That stops me. Most lifetimes seem short relative to eternity, but that's not how it strikes me. What about having [?] a lifetime in eternity – eternal life.

And you have it in abundance. Why would I deny you this? You have all the time in the world. And more besides.

More than all the time in the world?

Eternal life is not the time bound. It is.

Time can stop and life can go on?

Outside of the time box anything is possible.

It's just a constraint, I remember.

And it's very convenient. It allows you to grow. All-that-is becomes something and the some-things become somethings and the somethings become everything.

And the everything re-unites with the all-that-is.

Quite. And there's something else here too: you can have it both ways. You can reunite with the all-that-is and still be something,

We can know ourselves as though for the first time.

And in knowing yourself you know me.

For we are one, so what has eternal life.

I do. We do. You can become us.

That feels like ceasing to be myself.

And how does that feel?

If you had asked me a decade or so ago, it would have been scary, now it's sublime.

Of course, you can become yourself. Or something else.

How can I become something else?

You are not your self. Haven't you realised? You are not your self any more than you are your hands or your feet. Your self is just a vehicle.

So what am I?

Do you not know? Have you not realised? Let me introduce this gently...

Go on.

You are the created.

OK, so far.

And you are the creator.

I thought that was you.

On Life, Love and Loss

Welcome home. Who else did you think you were?

A hapless earthling, an actor in a play directed by someone I barely know; a mystery.

You are all of those things. Would you accept it if I said that you are a part of the creative force?

I am waking up to that.

And who or what is the creative force?

It is you. So you are it, this is it, there is nowhere else to go?

There are many rooms in this mansion.

But wherever I go, it is you?

Who did you expect? Actually, I am a reflection of you.

This is getting weirder. I thought you were the unchanging.

I am.

So how come you are different?

The only me you meet is the me you are ready to meet. You cannot me outside of your understanding of me.

So it is me who limits our relationships?

What's your choice?

I choose not to limit it: or at least I choose not to limit it more than I need to at any moment in time, in order to make sense of it, so I like gradual expansion.

Which is exactly what is happening.

So I am in charge.

You always were.

Amazing really, I am beginning to get the hang of this living thing.

You are.

18. Talk about Love

It feels OK, the whole thing feels OK, the known and the unknown. It makes more sense to me.

The sense it makes is limited by your senses.

If my senses were perfect, everything would make sense.

How else could it be?

So a key goal is to go on expanding my senses.

Awareness is awareness. Love is the key.

And the principal obstacle to love is fear, even greed is really a form of fear, and even killing is really a form of fear.

And what creates fear?

Ignorance, misunderstanding, lack of trust, absence of faith.

Absence of love.

So love is the antidote.

Be loving, always and everywhere; ask what would love do now.

Love would sense. Love would be sensitive. Love would be aware. Yet however loving we are, it could only be an echo of the divine love. Can we not borrow your love?

It is my love.

What do you mean?

To give love you have to receive love. You can only give what you have. Get better at receiving love, know that you are loved, and experience love.

We tend to think we don't deserve love, we certainly don't deserve your love, we are miserable sinners.

And you are ...

Miserable sinners!

Who are deeply loved, always, everywhere, world without end. And you don't experience yourself as a miserable sinner.

I am a joyful creator.

Be a channel for my love.

I seek to see, sense, feel, the joy in every moment, and to reflect that. At the same time, I aim to connect with the divine in each other that can feel that joy. I hope to sense some effect, some response, some understanding that there has been a connection. But even so, I feel it, and that is enough.

And is it enough for you?

There seems to be a great deal of confusion in the world. A shortage of clarity, our focus is on doing and having, rather than being loved and loving. We focus on being unable to do what we feel we should, and on being unable to have what we want. We aren't aware of where we could be. Maybe it's better to focus on how we could be.

Act like a magnet. You are magnetic: you are driving all of this stuff to you. Be aware of your magnetism.

But then, can I do more?

You can transmute it: turn darkness into light.

By connecting with the light that is already there.

19. Interacting

Thank you for this time and this place, thank you for you, thank you for me.

I am delighted to be here.

The question feels like this: what's the focus? And I would like the answer to be: listening.

Listening.

To you who makes the paths straight.

When you know where you are going.

I am coming towards you.

And …

I am experiencing more of who I am and more of who you are partly by realizing who I am not and who you are not.

And who aren't you?

I am not this or that thought, this or that emotion, this or that set of cells, I am the experiencer.

You are that: Influencer and Experiencer, I.E., that is.

I am the observer and are you not the observer of the observer?

You are more than the observer and I am more than the observer of the observer.

And you are an influencer and experiencer too?

I work with you. I am with you, I experience what you experience, how can I experience what is not?

I influence what you influence. Your influence is through me.

Don't you also influence us as influencers?

When called upon.

By whom?

By you.

Would you give me an example?

Suppose you ask me to make you more aware of my presence, or to guide you along the right path, or to shower you with blessings. Why will I not do that? You will I not do that? You will sense more presence, feel more guidance and receive more blessings, and all of that will influence you.

You could be even more fundamental, you could ask me to influence your asking.

That sounds like a good place to be.

And you already have more awareness, more guidance and more blessings, for myself and for others. And let this spread through humankind.

Who am I to be writing this stuff?

You are part of my creation. You are not incapable of this. The capacity is here.

So I can get on with it?

We can get on with it.

20. Politics

Let's talk about politics, a subject about which I have become confused.

> You are seeing more than one point of view.

Confusing.

> Yes, confuse.

Meaning to pour together. OK, maybe we can pour together. I want to ask, what's the role of Government?

> You choose.

There isn't a particular role that Governments should fulfil?

> What do you think?

I think that if you didn't have a Government, another Government would step in and become the Government. So I guess we will always have a Government.

> Until you pour together.

So we could do without Government?

> What do you think? Do you think there is a Government in heaven?

You're in charge in heaven.

> And I am not in charge here?

It doesn't feel like that, except

> Except when it does.

In heaven there are more constraints?

> No, in heaven there is more freedom. Actually you are totally free everywhere, you just don't live it. So there's no Government in heaven.

I have explored the word Government. It's from the Greek Kubernan, meaning to steer the ship, maybe we could steer the ship ourselves.

Pour together.

How do we change our politics?

Stop treating the other as other.

So that?

You stop competing and start loving. See yourself in everyone else and there's no sexism, racism, ageism, and there's no violence. Why would you violate yourself?

So we have to redefine our interest.

Redefine who you are.

Who are we?

You are we, you are one, you are one: constantly interchanging thoughts and emotions, molecules and bits and pieces with one another. You are flow.

We're us.

You are more than you think you are.

We are explorers.

21. Darkness

Another week begins. What will it bring?

That's a matter of choice.

How does that work?

Through your intent: as previously expressed, as it is expressed now, as it will be expressed.

And my will is my choice?

Your choice is your will, except when you don't. So often you say, I want this but it won't happen, more love in the world, for example, or you don't even say you want it, you've let go of it entirely.

Because we don't think it will happen.

And it won't, for so long as you aren't wiling it. When I ask, you say you do want to go in a direction, but you are taking the other way.

We're sat by the side of the road, going nowhere, we're wrapped up in the deluge of negativity that passes through the media, and infiltrates human consciousness; there's so much of it, so much of the time, we think it is normal. It's the way it is.

And it is the way it is.

Doesn't it take a huge effort to find another way?

You've already found it.

Doesn't it take a huge effort to practise another way?

Staying the way you are consumes a lot of energy, going round and round in circles consumes a lot of energy, and the negativity makes you very heavy. But there is a lighter path.

Where is it?

It is the lighter path, you can feel your way because the lighter path feels lighter.

Where is it?

It is everywhere. It's all around you, it's within you. It's in every lighter thought, it is in every emotion. It is in every lighter action.

But suppose there is no lighter thought, emotion or action?

When you don't sense the lighter path, notice you have strayed off the path. Look around for the lightest thought you can find. If there is still nothing, stop walking.

And?

Let light into your life, let it into your being, it is better to stop walking than to walk in the wrong direction.

I remember, I am a being of light. It still feels hard to me.

The light feels hard to you?

No, not the light. The darkness, being in the darkness feels hard. The whole physical world feels hard, most physical matter is!

And you would rather be?

Spirit, pure spirit.

And yet you are working with the world for a reason. You are attracted to it and it to you. You resonate.

And what is the reason?

To experience yourself afresh.

Surely also to experience myself as I am not.

To make choices.

And in the process to create.

Yourself anew.

22. Suffering

Sooner or later we have to talk about suffering. What is the cause of suffering?

> Choosing darkness over light. Resisting the light. Preferring darkness.

But when I suffer at someone else's hand, have I chosen darkness?

> Yes, you could have chosen only light.

I don't get this, I don't get this at all.

> Let me explain. Light conquers darkness, when you are confronted by darkness, what normally happens?

I become fearful.

> Right, you chose darkness.

That's me choosing darkness?

> What do you think fear is?

The biggest problem in the world today.

> And what are you going to do about it?

Banish all fears!

> Starting with yourself.

Fair enough, so when I notice a fear, what should I do? Send it away?

> What do you normally do with fears?

Oh, I let it get into me, into my gut, and it spreads a paralysis, so I don't act, and then I have a battle to take the action.

> Consuming a lot of energy. You could save a lot of energy if you choose light instead of darkness.

An altogether more elegant approach. OK, I have some worry-busting to do.

23. Flying

It was a good day, thank you. But it feels like I am more aware of the progress I make and less aware of the regress. It's strange: I notice spiritual presence but I don't easily notice its absence. When I am moving forward I am on the crest of a wave and can see, when I am in the trough I cannot see – all I can see is water.

And where are you now?

Halfway up the side of a wave.

And what would bring you up the wave?

Getting still, sensing, listening.

You can always know the way. Just get back in touch. If you don't know the way, that's a signal that you are out of touch, just get back in touch.

What about fear?

Fear is another signal that you are out of touch. Be fearless.

The Bible, for example, says again and again, do not worry, do not fret, do not let your heart be troubled. That's interesting, the idea of letting our hearts be troubled, as though that is something we do.

All the time. You let your heart be troubled all the time.

How can we not? An image comes to mind of a heart surrounded by light. Can we aid our hearts in this way?

You can aid your hearts in lots of ways. You can protect your whole being by placing white light all around yourself.

Is that it?

Be aware of what's going on around you. Be aware of what's happening in your energy field. Notice cause and effect.

Energy field?

Everything is energy, and all energy radiates an energy field. Even a rock is alive. Notice how you are dancing with the world, you are not impervious, you are porous. When you entered a room and felt a bad atmosphere, how did you feel?

Bad of course.

Exactly. But having noticed that bad atmosphere, you could have started to transmute it.

How?

Be rock steady. Observe the negativity. What you see is out there, not in here. Now choose how to handle it. You have externalised it.

I would like to radiate a soothing balm. Sometimes, I would like to blast the bad atmosphere with supercharged light.

And why don't you?

I am still feeling my way.

Do as you feel.

You mean I should start to fly.

And how will you feel as you soar?

And though I am being myself.

It's time.

24. Shine

Thank you for that, thank you for your guidance, thank you for each momentous moment.

Every moment can build momentum. Life is dynamic.

So I want your guidance now.

You have so many choices. Think about them, feel about them. Conjure up wonderful outcomes you haven't even begun to think of. Why do you keep thinking small?

I usually work within the confines of experience.

And so you repeat yourself. You are free: you know that, don't you? So allow your choices to unlimited. Stop aiming to be average.

The herd mentality! I think that I am seeking more but it feels like I keep getting pulled back, like mental gravity, if such a thing exists, and I am back on the ground again.

Why don't you believe in yourself?

I believe I am sometimes brilliant … I experience flashes of brilliance, but am deeply flawed too. Like a diamond, that shines brightly if you hold it in just the right way, but otherwise dull.

So I will hold you.

Does this mean I can transcend my negative conditioning, my occasional crippling self-doubt and shine?

Shine, Nigel, shine, and everyone else too: this is my gift.

Wow, your gift is that we shine, your gift is you will hold us, or we are your gift to yourself?

All of the above. And who else is there?

I am you as you are me and we are altogether, as it has been observed.

Again and again.

The truth is plain.

The truth is wonderful, amazing, enlightening, and right here now.

Right here, right now.

There is nowhere else to be.

And the truth will set me free.

Sense the truth, live the truth, be the truth.

And the truth is right.

And the truth is light.

Truth is what is. How can it not be true?

You are free but you behave as though you are not free, so you are not being true to what is. You live within an illusion. You are given abundant health and you damage your health: that is not being true to your inheritance. You are wonderful and you behave as though you are trivial, you are not being true to your potential, not even who you really are.

So I should slip of the cloak of rubbish that I have been shouldering and stride forth.

Realise who you are, realise who you are not, let go of who you are not.

25. Experiencing God

How do I know this isn't an illusion?

> How do you know all of life isn't an illusion?

Because I see, hear, smell, taste and touch. In short, I sense it.

> And you can sense me. You can be more or less aware of my presence. Anyway, all of life is an illusion.

Meaning?

> Meaning's key. Everything you see is an expression of something else, it is just manifestation, it means.

Meaning?

> It was meant to have meaning.

When something doesn't make sense the problem is probably with the senses.

> What is, is. What is sense is something else.

Different?

> Less than.

And that is the illusion of you. I sense less than you.

> So you see, as you experience me, I am an illusion.

Which doesn't mean you don't exist?

> On the contrary, I exist in everything.

So what am I experiencing now?

> An aspect of me: a point you can understand.

And this is illusion?

> Everything is illusion, temporary, temporal, less than fully experienced, here today, gone tomorrow.

But life continues. The experience of the illusion is real.

> There is the experiencer and the experience.

And what about what is experienced, the object that is the cause of the experience.

That is beyond you, except as you experience. By the way, be in no doubt, you are the cause of your experience.

The created and the creator, constantly recycling.

Recycling is what you do most of the time. Creation is more than that.

It's perplexing.

It is as it is.

Or as you said, your experience is your experience.

And the one who observes the whole thing.

You?

You can observe the whole process. You can be aware of yourself by stepping outside of yourself, as you understand yourself to be. As you become the watcher of your personality, you are no longer your personality.

You have moved to another place. Am I no longer the experiencer?

You are no longer wrapped up in that.

But I can still feel it.

You are less confused about who you are.

Am I no longer the creator?

At that moment, you may be watching the fruits of past creating. But eventually, this is a more powerful place from which to create.

Illusion.

Experience.

I can experience more than the illusion, I can experience reaching beyond the illusion.

You can experience creating, it may be more helpful to say you can become more aware that you are constantly creating.

26. Liberated

So what am I about?

That's your question.

It's a matter of self-definition?

There's no need to define the self. You are more than you imagine. Anyway, you don't have to start with: what am I about? You can start with "Who am I?"

I am being. I am being aware of who I am and who I am not.

Who are you not?

I am not limited, except by my sense of who I am, I am not time or space-bound, my ideas reverberate.

So what are you really about?

Expressing who I am.

And who do you choose to be?

Marvelous and wonderful and uplifting.

And why not?

No reason, now. What's the alternative?

So let it be glorious, let the gloriousness of creation shine through you.

As it will, except when we choose otherwise?

Your questions, your answers.

Can we do this naturally?

There is nothing more natural.

But it feels that we are struggling a lot of the time.

You struggle because you resist. Give in.

Give in?

Give inwards. Let your attention be within. Find the glory that you are. And then you can express it. When you find the glory within you also see it all around you because it is you. And you are seeing nothing more and nothing less than yourself.

It feels like there is nothing to do.

And how does that feel?

Strangely liberating.

And there is everything to be. Can you see doing is nothing more than a means to being, when it serves any purpose at all. If you no longer feel compelled to do anything in particular it may be you are sensing that being is enough.

Simply being myself.

What else could you possibly be?

Richer, poor, sick, well.

Illusions that have nothing to do with being.

But they affect the way we feel we are.

Because you are prisoners.

Conscious people of the world unite, you have nothing to lose but your wants!

Wouldn't you prefer to be free?

27. Jail Break

How do we get out of this prison?

Recognize you are the prisoner and the jailer.

And how do we play the role of jailer?

You imagine what you don't want. You imagine what you do want and then you imagine you won't have it, or that the process will be very difficult, and it duly is.

You want what you don't have and you get unhappy when you don't have it. As for what you do have, you are scared you will lose it, your house, your looks, even your life. You are particularly scared you will lose your life.

We deal with death by not talking about it.

Which hardly equips you to deal with it.

So how do we get out of the prison, by death?

You can get out of the prison here and now, of course that's the only time you can get out.

We have to stop wanting?

You have to let go.

Of what?

Of everything. Of your mind, of yourself.

We have to give everything away.

Realise you are just a steward: of your possessions, of your mind, even of yourself.

Is that all?

Give up your sense of separateness. Give up your sense of self and you may experience yourself as part of something infinitely greater.

When we realise we are a part, we can stop being apart.

Trade separateness for unity; but this is not false unity, this really is. The separateness is the illusion.

But what if we want to stay separate?

Actually it is not possible to fully experience this unity while you are still in the world, while you have a body, but your body isn't really separate. It is constantly exchanging matter with the surrounding world. Yesterday's body is, in part, "out there". Tomorrow's body is also, in part, "out there". But, of course, there really is no "out there".

28. The Way, the Life

Where to from here?

> There is nowhere to go, only here.

So what to do?

> Learn to be.

Aren't we always being?

> Hardly: think of doing as elastic. You can do more or less. So you can be more or less, and you can do your doing elegantly or inelegantly, and you can be your being, elegantly or inelegantly.

So we can be happy or unhappy, energized or frustrated, irritated, pretty much anything.

> And that's the key.

So we have choices, at any moment, to determine the nature of our being?

> If you are unable to do this, what are you able to do?

It seems so basic. We are wrapped up in having and doing and missing being, we are wrapped in the world and missing ourselves. How could we make such a basic oversight?

> How could you get insight?

Think I am getting insight now.

> And how do you do that?

Ask for it, be available for it, sense it, and be thankful for it, oh, and expect it, demand it. Somehow I feel this is our birthright. I mean, why would you put us here, with the ability to question if the answers could not be available to us, or, to put it even more starkly, why would we be here if there was no reason? The idea of a purposeless existence has never made any sense. The fact that I don't understand something doesn't mean it couldn't be understood. If it did, there would never be any learning.

A purposeless existence … and what if you define the purpose?

There is no purpose, then there is purpose. Purpose comes into life.

Purpose awakens you.

Our purpose is to awaken.

To experience, to know, to delight.

We learn through experience, we come to know, we delight in knowing, but what about the tree of knowledge, original sin and all that?

Do not learn to see yourself as disconnected, as separate from the whole, learn to see the whole, learn to experience yourself as absolutely connected with everything. This is, this is being, this is what it is.

Separateness isn't.

Separation is the veil.

It creates the possibility of billions or experiences, apparently separate, so it's convenient.

Unveil yourself as you are. And you see that we are. There's no more you and me, there's only us.

And the uni-verse is one word; literally.

As I have spoken.

You have spoken elsewhere. You have spoken in many religious texts.

I am speaking always. I "speak" everything into life.

And some of those texts – or the readers – claim exclusivity for you.

Exclusivity is akin to separateness. But if you look closely, you will see essentially, at the essence of what is being said, you will see they say the same thing.

"I am the way, the truth and the life".

When you become one, you become the way, the truth and the life. There is nothing exclusive about that. Anyone can be it. It is what you are called to be.

"No-one comes to the Father but via me".

No-one comes to me except that they become one with the way, the truth and the life. How else could it be? For I am one and the same.

Jesus is one with God, and the Buddha and the Prophets?

It is your calling, those who have ears to hear, hear me. This is your calling,

But we tend to say we have all parted, we have departed from your presence, and the way back is only for a few.

You have never departed from my presence, how could you? You may not have been aware of my presence. And expanding your awareness isn't that hard. It's not about effort.

When we do try, we try to expand our awareness of you. Tell me how.

Ask.

And it is given.

Allow me to give it to you.

Awareness of you is not ours to demand?

It is mine to give. It is the gift of life. Life like itself, do not deny me.

How do we do that?

When you say it shall not be so. When you say you shall not have it, when you say it is not here for you.

When you are quoted saying that kind of thing, there seems to be an implication that you are angry.

I am not. I am explaining how you deny me. I am explaining that when you deny me, you deny yourself me.

We deny your presence.

You deny the present. You deny the gift of life, you see the jug but not its content, you experience the bits of life but not its flow, you live in splendid isolation.

Splendid?

Well, it's not that bad, is it?

So what are we to make of the different religions?

Follow your calling.

And if we do not hear?

Start listening!

And if we think we have been listening?

Stop talking. Make some space. Quiet the mindless chatter around you, build silence into your days. Quiet the mindless chatter within you.

It is as though you have set it up that we can be noisier than you. We can drown you out anytime.

You choose your focus. I rarely butt in.

Rarely.

In extremis. Occasionally I deliver a wake-up call, understanding remains optional.

You keep pulling me off religions. You don't want to denigrate them.

There are many paths, but I am not a religion, think of religion as a means, not an end, do not be distracted by religion.

Do not practice religion?

Follow your path, follow your calling, use what works for you.

But don't try to make one religion better than another?

Don't try to make yourself better than another. Yourself, your clothes, your religions, are statements of who you are: uniforms. But there is only one form.

And what of New Age thinking?

Go with what works for you. You are constantly creating yourselves anew.

We are constantly re-expressing truths anew?

Inshallah.

Some of us have a problem with Islam.

Embrace it, embrace your brothers, embrace your sisters.

If we have convinced ourselves it is violent?

So don't be violent.

Many people, who call themselves Christians, have committed violence in the name of Christianity.

Turn the other cheek.

Jesus was pretty unambiguous on the most appropriate response to violence.

And the remedy is love. Love changes things. Love your enemy.

For your enemy is not your enemy. She is your friend in disguise!

And it is you who is wearing the disguise, let go of the scales in your eyes. See clearly. Everyone is your brother-sister as I am your father.

No favourites.

Do you not love all your children? Do you have favourites?

That sounds judgmental.

Love everyone. Love all. Love is all.

See the divine in everyone.

How can it not be there? It is there for you to see.

And in love we are free. Why do we do this comparative stuff?

Because you don't know how great thou art.

And then we fret, we worry that we are no good, in the absence of the awareness of our greatness, and then we worry that others are better than us, we decide they are worse, even though we don't belie it, to protect ourselves from our own judgment.

Often, you do believe it, because you don't know how great others art.

We react to the worldly in others, without sensing the divine in them, as we react to the worldly in ourselves, without sending the divine in ourselves.

Love one another as you love yourself.

Which would be an improvement on judge one another as you judge yourself, yet the divine is constantly present. It's evident in a baby's eyes.

And in an old man's eyes.

It's often evident when people say hello for the first time.

And when they depart this life. It's evident all the time, when you sense it,

So that's the task.

Always, everywhere, in every moment, this is happening, this is real, the challenge is here and now, this sense of who you are, this decision as to how you manifest, this realisation of who you are, is not something that need be left to the last moments of this life, or beyond, this is an opening. What will you? Are you open to it?

How can I decline?

You could say you have more pressing priorities: work to do, people to see, bills to pay.

And you don't press; but I know that is nonsense. Awareness of you can be there in the space around every word. In every breath, in the space between the in breath and the out, and so even as I go about my business, you are still, and in the stillness will I find you.

29. Fear

I feel a little bit anxious.

> Trust and be not afraid. Know that I am with you.

I am excited too. That this whole spiritual religious thing isn't a tomorrow thing: it's a here and now thing. It feels that much of my life I have been preparing or possibly postponing, with intermittent forays into the here and now, I've been playing a role, only occasionally expressing greatness. Now, I hesitate: your greatness, my greatness.

> Let's settle on our greatness.

How can I overcome this hesitation, this tentativeness? How can I be bolder?

> Forget yourself. To find yourself you must first lose yourself.

Easier said than done.

> The more you create space for me, the more aware you may become of me, the more willing you are to lose yourself, and the more space you create. But there's an easier way?

Which is?

> Ask for my help with this. How little do you ask! Imagine you have access to a God who will give you what you ask for: for what will you ask?

I often ask people something like this: three things that you would like to be different.

> And

They have seldom given it much thought. So you have handed the business of creation over to us, but there's a problem, we are confused!

> Out of your confusion can come fusion. I have let you be separate that we might come together.

And how do we do that?

I have shown you many ways. You can get better at co-creating.

By?

Giving your intent to me.

I thought I got clear on my intent and then handed that over to you. This feel like is am giving over the business of determining my intent.

Indeed you are. And do you not see that this is how you would like it to be?

Our intent, conjoined.

You keep pulling back from what you sense may not be my will for you, because you are constantly searching for my will.

I am trying to do the light thing!

So you get very tentative, hesitant, unsure when you do not sense that our will is aligned.

So that's a clue, that's feedback. But I thought your will was our will.

It is. I will go with it, but I will give you feedback, they are called feelings,

But I thought a lot of our feelings, fear, for example, were unhelpful.

Fear tells you that you are not in the right place. That you really don't need to be there, it's time to move on.

Let me see if I have this. I am worried that someone will take my car. Imagining … because of that I become fearful. That's because I am in the wrong place. How?

You are imagining someone will take your car, try imagining your car is surrounded by a protective light, now, whether your car stays of goes is fine, it's perfectly OK. And you know this because you have faith.

And if the car goes?

How do you know that won't be the perfect outcome? You don't. It may be. If you are walking in faith with me, it is.

So if I have fear, it's a clue I am in the wrong place, emotionally, I need to be somewhere else, but what it I am confronted by a sabre-toothed tiger?

Then it is especially important you have no fear. Knowing you are absolutely and divinely protected has the effect of summoning it up. You are in the co-creation business.

And you are constantly giving feedback.

Who else did you think was doing this?

The devil?

There is nothing that I have not created?

So you created the devil?

You imagine all kinds of things.

And through our imagination we make them real?

You can have the experience of being apart from me instead of being a part of me, you can create illusions.

I sense a hesitancy. Now I really want to pull back. We must focus on what we do want.

Align. Co-create. It's your call.

30. Flower

I am trying to find my way. When I have found my way, I would try to stay there but lose it and in doing so I seem to lose it that I have lost it. So the first challenge is to be aware that I have lost my way, that awareness seems to be a benign place to start, it feels like a blessed place.

Then you haven't lost it at all, sensing blessing is a sign you are on your way,

Sometimes it feels so hard. It feels like I am crying out in the wilderness.

When you cut yourself off from me.

There's a paradox. It feels to me that, on the one hand, you do have a preference for light, love and laughter, and yet on the other you are completely imperturbable, as though it has no impact on you of any kind, as though it doesn't really matter,

In the end, it doesn't really matter, along the way, it may make quite a difference to you,

It's not the result, it's the journey.

You are on a journey, are you not?

And on this journey, I am changing, that is what the journey is.

You are coming into flower.

And the flower is there in bud.

Perfectly formed.

So you don't mind how our petals fall?

It's your journey.

There are millions more species on the planet. We humans tend to focus on our own welfare and the people around us, and to a lesser extent on other human beings. Apart from our pets, we little value of other forms of consciousness.

It's their journey.

We say thou shalt not kill, but for, say, cattle, it's a different story.

There are places where cattle are sacred.

It's wrong to kill cattle?

You have to do the best you can with the information you have.

When, say, an insect is about to be killed, or is being killed, I feel that.

So behave appropriately. If you feel it, stop doing whatever it is that creates the feeling.

And that's up to us to choose.

You are choosing it, day and night.

And the insects: What about them? They go off to heaven?

What do you think?

I think consciousness is never created not destroyed: it just changes form.

It separates and unifies.

And I am on the unification path?

Is that what you wish?

I am not sure I am ready for unification quite yet, but I am happy to be on the path. I quite like having it both ways: separate and joined.

And so you are.

Yes, this is exactly where I am: on the path, knowingly, striding forth: progressing pausing, regressing, going, hanging out, watching the world go by; going round in circles, having a wonderful time. Thank you very much.

It's my pleasure.

Meaning?

I am here too.

31. A Sense of Being Guided

Talk with me about guidance.

How does it feel when you are guided?

An upward glance, an intake of breath, a momentary pause, precedes the guidance, and then it's there. It's difficult to catch what happens in the instant, it's just there, here I mean.

And how does it feel?

Beautiful, elegant, simple, and effortless: like finding there is a present in your hands that you didn't know was there.

Would you like to be guided all the time?

I feel your guidance is there all the time, ready to be given.

And yet you don't ask.

Not so much.

So how would you like to be guided all the time?

That's a big question: part of me would like to have a little wriggle room, being my confused self has certain consolations. And I wonder if, after a period of constant guidance, would I be able to revert?

Would you want to?

I don't think so. But it could happen without me noticing, but then I don't notice so much, the idea is growing on me.

The sense of being guided is more commonplace.

OK, I've thought about it, I'd like as much guidance as I can easily take. I realise the constraint is nothing to do with you, I am going to ask in the morning, at lunchtime, in the afternoon, in the evening, and at night for the following day, most days, minimum.

And how will you do that?

"Guide me this day", I shall ask, or something similar. And the request will be wrapped in a perfect faith that the guidance will be there. I think that if the overall guidance is there, the specifics will fall into place. The challenge with asking specific questions is they are often the wrong question. Or it's the right question at the wrong time, or there would be a better question. I feel it's important to start at the general level.

This is quite an adventure you know. Each time I sit down to write I have little idea what is going to come up, nor am I certain anything will.

You take quite a lot of convincing.

This feels a lot easier than other forms of writing, just an effort, or sorts to get myself into the right place, and then it is over to you, like riding a bike: a push to start and then keep balanced.

You've been preparing.

Intermittently, occasionally.

For a very long time.

32. Miracles

I am here, perhaps a little late, just present, but ready to be guided.

> Is that enough?

I don't know: it feels like it could be a start.

> I will guide you.

Well, thank heavens for that.

> If you will listen.

Help me to listen through the day. Help me to listen at each juncture. Help me to listen in every moment. I'd like to continue.

> For what purpose?

To develop my understanding and to enjoy your company, most especially to see what insight may be prompted, currently, my challenge is that it all seems to make so much sense.

> And is that such a bad thing?

No, what words of encouragement would you offer?

> Do your best.

That's not original. I've been asking for some time.

> Be bold. Realise what you are scared of.

Not fulfilling my mission, straying from the path, falling in battle.

So do fulfil it. Stay on the path. And sense your complete protection.

I am protected?

> Not a hair on your head can be hurt.

Without your permission.

> Without yours.

Can we talk about miracles?

Isn't existence miraculous?

Yes it is, and sensing the miraculous in every moment is – I think – a great place to start.

What's a miracle to you?

Something that defies the laws of physics, that is outside all expectation.

Well, then a miracle wouldn't happen. If it's a law of physics, it's a law, and if it confounds, all expectations, it wouldn't happen.

For a miracle to happen there must be expectation?

More than that, there must be intent, and the force of that intent must be enough to overcome all the negative intent that it won't happen. And why would you want to know more about miracles?

Because I would like to broaden my understanding.

You are not interested in performing miracles?

I don't want to put on that kind of show. I think it's a tricky path to tread. Yet if it will enable me, enable others to see things differently, to see real possibilities, then it may be something to consider.

Are you doing your best with this?

I'm not sure.

Where's your boldness. If I told you that you could perform miracles, would you?

I suppose if it felt right, if it felt that I had your permission, if I wasn't showing off in any way, I would.

If you were showing off, miracles wouldn't show up.

You would have to be with me every inch of the way.

Indeed.

I would have to maintain that awareness all the way through, like a tight-rope walker.

How could it be otherwise?

Having performed the odd miracle, Jesus is quoted as saying "Why are you amazed? You can all do what I do".

So why don't you?

Hey, there's your territory and there is our territory.

This is what I am telling you: there is one territory.

OK, I am ready to step up, incrementally, and perhaps much more slowly than is possible. I have to feel my way.

You all do.

Isn't it going to get a bit mad if there is suddenly an army of miracle workers?

Look around your world: does it need healing?

Yes.

And?

33. Brother

Tell me more about creating miracles.

What do you want to know?

How to perform them!

This will take a little time. First realise you are a constantly-creating being, we are in the creation business, there is nothing that has not been created. There will be nothing that will not be created. It is not in your nature to not create.

I'm doing it all the time?

You cannot not do it even for a moment. You already know something about how to do this.

Get myself focused, get myself clear, get my energy flowing nicely, get a bit passionate, see it, feel it, believe it, live it, stay with it until it's real.

You do know even though you don't always practice. And by the way, that's how you create miracles.

The same?

There's nothing to it.

I don't believe it.

And that's the problem.

There must be more. One can't simply click one's fingers and watch miracles come into being.

When you are one with being you can.

So there is more.

You have to be coming from a place of unity, not separation.

When I am one with the situation, when I am in alignment with it, I can, as it were, play with it. I can change it.

Yes you can.

That reminds me that when you want to win friends and influence people, you need to get alongside them, you need to be with them, before you really influence them.

> It's more than that. You are becoming one nor merely with that which has been created but also becoming one with that which has not yet been created.

In other words, becoming one with you, for are you that which has not yet been created?

> You become with that part of me, you are using that part of me, and that is well put.

Yet choice comes into it, in that moment of creation, we are choosing a specific outcome.

> Amen.

It seems to me that there are miracles of different sizes.

> There is what you believe and there is what you do not believe.

That makes the difference?

> Think about it, when did you last really believe something would be, and it wasn't?

When I have certainty I am there?

> Hope is not enough. Take responsibility. Take charge. This is you calling.

You don't think we are trying?

> You are not aligning as you could.

When you are riding a bicycle it doesn't quite work to try to lean to the left, then try to lean to the right, it's more like you feel it.

> You don't think we are ready?

> You don't think you are ready, but readiness is a relative term. I don't advise you to walk a high-wire until you can balance well.

So we have to practice, that feels OK.

> You could up the tempo, you could practice more than you have been.

Indeed, it's only recently that I've really committed to and followed daily practice.

And the results: have you sensed a difference?

We're here. I could do so much more.

You could experience so much more being.

This is all rather encouraging, and it sounds rather straightforward, and experiencing much more being sounds like nothing but upside. But doesn't the spiritual path involve a lot of giving up.

What's your experience?

Well, I am trying to have it both ways by leading an active life within the world while developing my inner life.

And

It seems to be working find, after a fashion?

So are you giving up a lot?

There is s sense in which I am giving up, to an extent. I am giving up the result, in the sense that it is a shared result, I am not quite "giving it up" to you, but there is a feeling of partnership. I am, as it were, looking up a little more.

And how does that feel?

Beautiful, and strangely empty, uncluttered, a place of creation; and there is absolutely no sense of pressure to give anything up to you; just a voluntary loosening of the reins.

You don't need to hold the reins at all.

Now that feels kind of scary.

Think about it. When you are at your absolutely most inspired, what is going on?

I'm not thinking at all, I'm just receiving.

And when you are playing a sport well?

No thought, no time for thought, just being there.

So, do you want to hold the reins?

I'd like it to be so that I didn't need to hold the reins for sustained periods of time.

And

I don't? OK, I don't, which doesn't mean everything goes to hell and a hand basket.

Quite the opposite: If you hand things over to me in the expectation everything will go to hell and a hand basket, you prevail. Don't you see that trust changes everything?

I see that, in the moment I have allowed for reflection, I have often wanted to feel able to trust, but it is also true that I have usually sought my own counsel. I have doubted the existence of any kind of God without seriously investigating it.

By starting a conversation?

And even when I have subscribed to a religious point of view, I have rarely entertained the idea of direct contact. I suppose it seemed that it would be too much, and so it could not be.

But you have noticed.

And even when I've noticed something, so extraordinary that I am entirely satisfied it is you, or a form of you from another realm, still I haven't set about developing the relationship. But hang on a minute, neither have you.

I am going at your pace.

So we are managing our relationships with you. We don't seem to be much better at it than managing our relationships with one another.

On your off days, you imagine others are like yourself and then you damn them for it; you imagine I am like you and then you damn me, and then you think I will let you down.

Aren't there lots of people who feel let down?

And what do you say?

I say, let's build: capability, hope, trust, optimism, energy, balance,

115

the works. I say, when people feel let down, let's be the change.

And changing business too?

Yes: lives that have meaning, working lives that have meaning, businesses that are committed to noble purposes.

Like making money?

I see nothing necessarily wrong in making money, and nothing necessarily right either. Money is a means to an end.

In many people's eyes it has become the end.

And the problem about that is real ends are cast to the winds. One powerful political ad showed various kinds of environmental damage and then said, "It doesn't have to be like this".

And you don't have to be like that.

34. Reflections

You are like a reflection of me.

> You are getting to know yourself.

Like the wisest big brother I could have, who gives it to me in terms I can immediately understand, but I see you are so much more than that, you express yourself in terms each individual will understand.

> Where that is their will.

And I see I am so much more than the little me I have more usually experienced: a miracle from top to bottom.

> You are getting more of it.

Thank you for continuing to be so responsive.

> Even when I am not.

Meaning

> I don't respond in the ways you don't expect me to.

Even then, I have an idea: you've heard it before, I've heard it before, but I've never really meant it. Let's have peace on earth, really, let's have it. Let's have enough food and drink for all.

> You do.

Let's have really good education available to all. The difference is I really mean it, I am not saying these things as a demand, a complaint, or in any way negatively, I just mean it, pure and simple. Let's go for it.

> You've made up your mind.

It's taken a while. The insight is more about the process.

> OK, and can you see it, can you feel it, can you sense it becoming real?

I am working on it, intentionally.

35. Waiting

I wait upon you.

> And I am waiting for you.

But I am here and ready.

> I am waiting for the real you to live your dream. When will you?

It feels to me that I am moving along a tunnel, that I can sense it, I can almost touch it.

> Actually, it is coming towards you. You are drawing it.

So, I am ready?

> You know how ready you are. Why have you been holding back for so long?

Fear of failure, I suppose. It's less risky to move with the herd.

> You have seldom moved with the herd. And, incidentally, it is easier to be brilliant.

That is one of the secrets, isn't it, intending to be brilliant, from time to time, I have thought of a book that would be called *"Brilliance for beginners"*.

> You have had many potentially brilliant ideas. And my challenge is: where are they? You have a contribution to make: why aren't you making it?

I am contributing in lots of small ways.

> It is time to live your dream. Can I count on you?

Now you are coaching me. Alright, yes, come what may.

> I am waiting upon you.

36. Success

OK, I have faith.

In what?

In us, in being, in presence, I am more aware of the magic in each moment. There's a game I like to play, when you see someone who you haven't seen for, say, a day, imagine that you haven't seen them for a year, and then see how it feels as you great them. Or if you see some birds flying, imagine that birds have never been known to exist, and you are now seeing them for the first time, how different.

All you have to do to experience more of the world it stop taking it for granted.

In a book about happiness it is suggested that a second ice cream won't give you as much pleasure, but it can. We could call it the F5 (refresh) technique.

The F5 Refresher.

I'm more aware that I am alive, that life is filled with possibilities.

That life is endless.

Meaning?

Every ending is a beginning.

Every end is a means?

Means are ends. There's no difference. There is just one process.

And we are in it.

You are it.

I am not sure where this conversation is going.

Do you trust me?

Well, yes.

And do you know where your life is going?

Not really, a vague sense.

Sharpen your senses.

They are still rather flaky.

And do you trust me?

How can I not?

Enjoy the moment. That's enough.

There must be things I haven't asked you.

You can ask anything. Were you planning not to do so?

37. Feeling Success

Let's talk about success.

Which is?

Well, that's where it starts.

With what?

With a definition of success.

Don't define it, it's unlimited.

But at least get a sense of it.

Success is a feeling, start with that, finish with that, keep it all the way through.

Success can't be measured in results?

The results are an indication of the feeling, mostly your feelings are awry, they aren't helping you accomplish whatever you want to accomplish.

You are saying what we wish to accomplish is irrelevant.

Not irrelevant, secondary. Work at the level of feeling, Get your antennae going. Feel it out.

This feeling thing, it seems to be about more than how we feel. Is it about how it feels, for example, the result?

It is about how the whole thing feels. You pull all of that together and then you notice how that feels.

Where are feelings?

They are everywhere.

All around us, inside us, between us?

Everywhere

Can they be concentrated in particular places?

You, for example, are a repository of feelings, you receive, you store, you transmit.

And we transmute.

And sometimes you recycle old feelings, on and on.

Which is unnecessary?

You could be here now.

We could stop playing yesterday's tapes. Are you suggesting there's no value in memories?

Play them when you want to. Allow yourself to come into the equation. Realize you are the operator of the machine, not the machine. That would be success.

We think that matter isn't conscious, animals aren't conscious they are conscious, and we are.

Now it is time to run your consciousness. You are the programmer not the programme.

But isn't there a higher level still?

Surely: co-creation.

Yes, we work it out together, with much, much greater harmony, and how do we do that?

You know, you listen, you feel, and you even talk.

And isn't there a higher level still?

There's more and more closeness, and then there's unity. And the closeness produces more and more alignment.

So success without alignment isn't such a success after all?

Keep shining through.

This is mad, really. I have been living my life without the benefit of a dialogue that I now sense was there all the time, I have been running this way and that, expending energy, without knowing where I was going, and usually without getting there.

How does that feel?

Well, it has felt engaging, exciting, frustrating, debilitating, re-energising and sometimes joyful.

So it wasn't so bad. But how does this feel?

Preferable, sensible, surprisingly practical, aligned and joyful; and satisfying at an altogether different level.

And would you like to stay?

I'd like to build this into my life so it becomes as automatic as breathing. With every in-breath you inspire me. It takes life to another level of being. It's not just about unity with you – though that would be enough – it's about unity with everything, my God, everything makes sense. Literally, everything makes sense. I feel like there is a wave of love cascading through the universe.

It is the universe. Welcome to it.

38. Unifying with

Where to next?

Are you listening? There is only here.

How can we make the path plain?

Start with love; Always and everywhere. Within this world, build awareness.

I think the key is for people to become aware that they are aware and also aware that there is much of which they are not aware.

Become aware of awareness.

Awareness is elastic. You can be more or less aware, but there is a real shift when you are aware of awareness.

When you are observing the is-ness. And when you are an observer you are a creator.

Become aware of yourself as a creator of creation.

You mean become aware of the constant act of creation, the non-stop manifold process,

So the path includes a shift from seeing ourselves as the created to seeing ourselves as creators.

Experience yourselves that way.

As we become aware that we can make conscious choices, we can knowingly select outcomes. From being the experience of others, in other words not really experiencing anything, we can become aware we are the experiencer, then we can observe ourselves as the creator of the experience.

And then sense that you are nothing. Nothing more than a spark of consciousness that hasn't realised consciousness, you see yourselves as separate, but nothing could be further from the truth. Experience oneness: you are part of the delightful interplay.

And how do we get that?

Be the book you are looking at. Be the thought that crosses your mind, be the next person you see, you already are, you are just developing your sense of being, a being which already is.

Well, that should be pretty easy.

It is. Start unifying: everyone, everywhere, everything. you tend to imagine spiritual practice is very difficult, that it is the preserve of the devotees, that one must be initiated before one can start, but I am beside you always.

There is no difficulty with spiritual practice?

If love is your intent, none whatsoever. And as you know, I walk beside you: what could be easier?

Certain hurdles remain. We imagine we already know and so we are not interested in knowing more because we are not interested in seeing any more because we suppose we already see, we are not interested in hearing more because we suppose we already hear what there is to hear.

So when someone says, "I have been talking with God", or "I have been seeing Jesus" or "I know why we are here", defence mechanisms spring into place. The speaker is excluded and the possibility that they have knowledge is excluded too.

What do you not know?

We are like someone who is at a party, and is having a fairly good time, who is dimly aware that she doesn't remember who invited her, nor when the party will finish – a common occurrence – nor what form of transport may be available. On reflection she doesn't know where the transport would take her to anyway, nor why she came to the party in the first place.

In other words, we don't know where we have come from or where we are going, why we have come or when we are leaving. Most of us are prepared to bury further investigation by simply assuming we came from nowhere, and we are going nowhere and there is no reason. But they know they don't know, they've just decided not to check it out. Others decide they have joined a group with the answers. Even though they don't understand themselves, as a matter of faith they have decided not to have faith in themselves but to surrender it to others.

And in what do you have faith?

In existence, in being, in us, in you.

And not in yourself?

There is an unguided me, I have faith in guided me, though unguided me has been a lot of fun.

'Unguided you' is a has-been?

I would like it to be that way. I would like to be accessing your guidance in every moment of every day, and acting accordingly. I don't suppose for a moment that is realistic.

Because ...

It would represent a big change.

And you are not interested in change.

No, change is my middle name, so to speak, it's hard-wired into me, let's go for it, even if my odds of success are virtually zero.

And you are not committed to the process.

No, it feels to me that there is no other process, and that this is inevitable. It's a one-way travellator.

You sense my commitment to enable you.

And boy do I feel enabled, but I am not quite there yet, am I?

You are waking up.

I feel ready to become much more awake. I feel it is happening. Thank you for your help.

39. Separate

This whole unexplored world. Even this whole, unseen world, worlds within world, so much.

Why are you here?

I am here to strengthen my connection with you and to see what good may come of it, and to give you thanks, I misunderstood the practice of thanks giving, of course, I had come to the view there wasn't much point in giving you thanks because you are completely complete, so to speak. But of course, thanks giving benefits the giver, so giving you thanks can be a great benefit.

And how do you do this?

Easily, innocently, any time, with little or no preparation, spontaneously.

Do you not see that all spiritual practices are easier than you think?

I think this is the challenge for many of us: actually to practice to any significant extent. .Someone practices 24 minutes a day, which sounds a lot, until he observes that is just $1/60^{th}$ of the day. Another writer talks of turning everything into ritual, and this feels very appealing, I would like to really enhance my performance and move up to the next level.

And why would you like to do that?

I think it is a bit like the mountaineer who says "Because it is there", so I shall say "Because you are here" and if that does seem to be too much based on supposition, I shall say "Because I have noticed that I am here, and this doesn't entirely make sense to me"

Because you aren't. When you say, "I am here" it is your illusion that keeps you separate.

So when Renee Descartes said "I think therefore I am" he might as well have said "I think therefore I am separate".

Unity is everything, being is primary, while thinking and feeling are secondary.

Some people will think I am saying, "Stop thinking".

We are.

And they will point to all the gains, the scientific advances, made by thinking.

But they were all made by stopping thinking,

You mean, we – whoever – had done our analysis, our research, whatever, and then we simply received the breakthrough.

Tune in to the knowledge that is already there.

But you aren't saying, never think?

What do you think? Are you thinking right now?

Yes, it often feels like I have to think of my lines, yours come through automatically.

Even yours, your thoughts, when they finally come, that bit is really effortless, why don't you go to the last bit quicker? You waste a lot of energy.

I am all ears, please teach me.

Get better at listening.

For you, listening isn't an occasional thing, I get the impression it's a regular thing.

I listen all the time.

40. A Life Tourist

Thank you for all the glorious things in my life: an abundance of wonder.

It's my pleasure.

Yes, I get that. It would be your pleasure because you experience what we experience.

I am the experience.

And you would have to be, being the source of everything, and the everything of which you are the source.

And I have to be.

Because you are the "I am", you are being, there is no unbeing for you to unbe. But within the time-box the normal reality rules do not apply, in the place we have being and unbeing.

Creation and destruction, and recreation and so it goes on.

And on and on, which is fine except when you get caught up in it and mistake it for the real thing.

Even then there is glory: there is glory in the confusion of reality and unreality.

Death and glory.

Glorious life everlasting, world without end.

When we transcend.

Which is what you are doing now, even in this minute, in this place, you are also outside of it, looking back in, from a place where you in reality are completely serene.

Yes, it feels like that is where I am. So you are saying I am outside the world, looking in?

You are real. You exist entirely independently of the world, you have a day pass.

I am some kind of tourist?

You can see, can't you, that it is only a temporary visit that you have made?

Have made, I am still having it, but I have felt like some kind of visitor for some time, now, almost an intruder, as though I have strayed into a garden where the grass is rather long, ah, I see I have strayed outside a garden into some kind of meadow, though I remain not far from the walled gate.

It is time to return.

41. Spreading

I start by presuming you are here, feeling that you must be, that you cannot not be, and that there is a readiness on your part to tune in and a lack of resistance on my part, if not much in the way of proficiency.

That is a good place to start.

So we are off, we can resume.

Anytime, all the time: why not walk with me all the time?

Amazingly, it feels like I forget you. Yet a residue of the interaction seems to linger. And I return.

Why would you return?

To ensure, at least, that the path I am walking is the path I should walk.

Which is

The path to enlightenment: receiving and giving nudges along the path.

How are you walking?

A little more surely based on an extraordinary assurance: that this is just how it is meant to be.

So your promise isn't in the future.

It's here now. I am here now. Now that's it.

Now is won. Now is one.

Yes, everything feels more connected, I am less like me, more like a ripple in a wave,

Which is where your physicists are getting to.

Aren't they missing consciousness?

Thought evolves.

It feels like we have a long way to go.

And that's OK, you have come a long way.

No pressure?

Can you feel it?

Problems in life come when we resist the flow, when we aren't in tune. I am finding it difficult to keep up with you.

Actually, you find if difficult when you don't keep up with me.

But how can I keep up with you?

It is I who keeps you up.

Let's do this thing together. In glorious awareness: of who we are, where we are and what we are, let's live in now.

Amen.

But this is not enough. I want to know how to spread the sense of your presence this deep assuredness around the world.

And you think you don't know how to do this?

Wow, I think that even if I didn't know – and I can't say I am sure I know the optimal path – it wouldn't rather because you know, and we can do this together, indeed, we will, now the whole thing looks completely accomplishable, so that's what we will do.

Co-creation. What are you waiting for?

42. What is the Problem?

This is quite a discipline, being here with you.

Would you rather not be?

No, I am very happy to be here regularly, it's just that I have to resist the temptation to be doing something else.

And you have turned this into a doing too.

Yes, it helps me to define it as an activity.

So where would you like to go now?

Here is fine, this subject, balancing spontaneity and discipline in the spiritual life, I have always been one for spontaneity but I am experiencing some of the merits of habit.

There's no contradiction, you can have both, always be spontaneously in the moment. This doesn't mean you can't have ritual. Ritual is a tool for spontaneity.

But do we need Churches?

You are in my Church. The world is my Church, what did you think it was?

So do we need specific places of worship?

What do you think?

They can be helpful, and they can be unhelpful, helpful when they provide really good spiritual training, unhelpful when they simply get in the way of authentic spiritual experience.

You need guidance. And most people hesitate to go directly.

They don't believe it. They don't believe you can go directly. They shy away from authenticity. They seek to stay within the herd, unaware that the herd is going nowhere.

The herd is evolving.

Painfully slowly, wouldn't joyfully quickly be rather more fun?

Have it your way?

For goodness sake, haven't we had enough of fear-based activities, politics and even religions? And haven't we had enough of freed-based economics and social structures? When will we ever learn?

So what is the problem?

Fear: and the fear can be replaced by love, because love and fear cannot co-exist. When you are in love you are fearless!

Love everyone, all the time, love everything. Be so filled up with love you cannot help it, make love who you are.

Wow, that's wonderful, but we are going round in circles.

Loving circles, and as you know, there's nowhere else to go.

And each time I circle, it all makes a little more sense, in every circumstance, I could choose love.

What matters is who you are. That determines everything. You determine everything through who you are.

And love is our true nature? And being unloving is our untrue nature.

You are evolving. You are becoming more comfortable with love.

Step inside love. I'd like to encourage other people to sit down and do this; talk with you. Imagine if millions of people did this, this could all upload it, it could all be available on the web.

A community.

Yes, a community of people in communion with you, as well as we are able, what an idea! It would be absolutely spontaneous, people could take what they want from it and the community can add; but there would be problems, some people might add unhelpful material.

So you would have rules, which would enable spontaneity within that framework.

What an idea, what an idea, well, you have knocked me out this time, extraordinary. As this developed I felt you were leading me.

Looking back at the text it looks like it's my idea, but I felt led all the way. It was as though I was leaning so far forward that I couldn't help but make progress, so the whole thing felt effortless. So thank you. I'll do it. I've had enough of not doing the big stuff. I'm ready to go large! There are some caveats: We have to be careful not to claim we have the truth, just a interpretation. We have to be respectful of different points of view.

43. Help

As we have the connection, and it feels as though I have struggled for many years to make such progress, how can we help others to make more progress more quickly?

> Answer their call. Make yourself available. Be there for them.

How can I answer their call if I don't know what it is?

> Listen, they are calling.

Do they hear themselves calling?

> At some level they sense their incompleteness, and this is nothing more or less than a yearning to be re-united with the divine.

Don't many of us find a sense of completeness with our families?

> Sometimes. Have you see what goes on in some of our families?

OK, so the yearning for you is purer, creating a purer response and a purer experience. I thought **you** answered their call.

> I do, but you asked to help. You can answer some calls.

Hmmm, not what I expected. I was looking for a whiz-bang formula, a form of words.

> Words are a poor representation of love, and that is what you have to give.

Isn't there more? Isn't it obvious we are going in the wrong direction, we are wrapped up in doing and having, and missing out on the experience of being?

> Are you?

Yes, I am enjoying the process of being, having and doing.

> So be it.

But my experience is many others aren't, they are leading hyperactive lives of quiet desperation; like hollowed out shells. I'd like them to call out more.

They are calling all the time. Why not respond?

How?

In every moment, bring a sense of completeness where there is incompleteness, bring wholeness.

Be thou whole!

I am, you are, it is, you know this to be true.

Incompleteness would not feel inadequate if completeness were not an option. Holiness is not an abstract, spiritual state, reserved for the devout: wholeness is a here and now thing.

You do not know who you are because you do not experience who you are.

But as we experience who we are, we come to know who we are.

Nothing, everything, not self, an interconnection, a temporary glitch.

I'm temporary.

As you know yourself now, temporary. As you come to know yourself, eternal.

I'm a temporary eternal being.

You're both. You're in and outside the time-box.

And what about the glitch?

You are so much more than that, but that's how you often experience yourself. Not quite fitting in.

That's because I want to change the world.

You are. And you are doing it by changing yourself.

Be the change we want to see!

What else?

That feels hard, aren't we all works in progress?

You have yourself, work on it.

So this is why I am here?

What else?

To be a great expression of yourself to enlighten the world, to be your servant.

It's your call.

But you know, you know everything.

My knowing your calling doesn't prevent you. It couldn't be otherwise, nothing can be that is not in my imagination.

So we are details in your imagination.

Where else did you think you were?

On our own, in a separate place, doing our own thing, cast off.

And yet you are here.

As though we're attached to you.

There is no way out.

Of your imagination?

Except to become the imaginer.

So that is our destiny.

But there are gradations of being, aren't there, between human beings and God.

You are evolving. You can become anything, everything, all that is, actually, you are just realising that's who you are, there is so much more to realise,

It feels like I am just beginning.

Isn't that exciting?

44. Practices

I want to suggest some practices, like asking yourself why am I here? I know the question is often talked about, but my sense is that it is seldom confronted, even laughed about, and confronting it can create some appetite for that path: if and when you realise you have absolutely no idea why you are here, that's a great place to be.

A great place.

Yes, because you can encounter some space, an opportunity, a place to move into. Awareness of ignorance precedes understanding. Keep on asking the same question over and over again.

Why not ask yourself: who am I? Or even, who do you choose to be?

Anyone can have this conversation?

This is your conversation, anyone can have a conversation like this.

At a time of their choosing.

Anytime works for me.

So what are we waiting for?

What have you been waiting for?

I have been wondering, I have been busy, I've been tentative. There's a lot to take in here. I haven't been bold. And most of the time, I haven't been undertaking any spiritual practice. It is only this year that it has become a daily practice.

And this provides the springboard.

It feels like it is all coming together, though not quite in the way I expected.

It is altogether.

Yes, I appreciate that, in as much as this is faith, it does not feel like a thing to be strived for or even hoped for, just a deep inner knowing.

One indivisible whole.

But what about when everything seems divided?

That's a clue that you are in illusion.

Step outside, love.

Step outside the illusion, step inside love.

And the feeling thing is really feeling. It feels like it is around my heart, there's a lot of lightness there.

Where else would you have it?

In and around everywhere.

So it is.

So when we see what appear to be divisions we don't have to heal divisions out there, we have to heal divisions in here?

You have to get yourself to a place where there are no divisions.

And from there everything seems perfect even when it isn't?

And from there you know that everything is perfect, from a snowflake to a planet.

Why do you bother with us when we so obviously don't get it?

You are more fun than you think, this is fun, isn't it? You are getting to know.

45. As Close as Breath

Guide me this day too. Be as close to me as my breath.

I am your breath.

OK, so that's granted, grant me consciousness of presence all this day. As these words come tumbling out, I can imagine anyone who may be reading them wondering, what is this?

It is everything. It is the difference between night and day, it is the light of my presence.

Surely it lifts everything, it changes everything, nothing is a threat, nothing doesn't flow. In the quietening of everything the virtual absence of everything is perfect peace. It is as though blessing is in me and around me.

You can partake of the blessing and you can shun the blessing.

Work with the light.

Walk in the light.

That's great guidance, thank you

Can you feel it?

How can I not? It is in me and around me, it is the Glory of God. You know, I am becoming rather convinced about this.

You've been convinced for some time.

I am expressing it more.

You are receiving it more. Let it flow? Can you not feel the flow?

I can hear the wind in the trees, the air, I can hear the silence of your presence, I feel a welling up of emotion inside me.

And this too shall pass.

46. Uplifting

I don't think I have stopped being human.

> You're not human.

I remember, I haven't stopped making mistakes.

> That's why I keep calling out to you. When will you come forward?

False modesty, fear of failure. The Gremlins haven't entirely gone.

> Oh yes they have. When you experience the presence of God, where are they?

In remission.

> Would you like to respond more positively?

Sometimes I feel I am losing my way.

> That is because it is not your way.

And I don't see far ahead.

> And you don't need to have to see ahead at all, except as you intend, what good would it do you?

I don't see the next step in my development.

> Because you can only really get it when you get it, until then it's mystery. But when you do get it, it's clear.

Yes, it is very clear, but certain mysteries remain.

> Until they don't.

The creation of the whole thing seems absolutely vast from where I am, but I am vast compared to say, a white blood cell. In any event, the scale is incredible.

> That is because you are within the scale, from outside those parameters there is no scale at all.

So separation into this and that provides an opportunity for vastness, and the same for time. Yet, if it's all illusion, you really could have an infinite amount of it. If there are no limitations, then you can have any scale at all.

And I do: so what's the mystery?

The mysteries seem to have receded, like an outgoing tide or an uplifting fog, but as the tidal fog goes, you will stay, won't you? I mean it wasn't just that I needed your presence to work my way through the mysteries.

You have only to open your heart.

47. A Part

Who am I? I am a vessel. This is different: answers are coming to me.. Just getting into gear, I guess. Why am I here? To be myself, I guess; and what is that?

That is what you are discovering: who you really are.

And who am I?

A part of me.

Not apart from you?

No, that is just the illusion.

The illusion that makes unification possible: without the illusion of separation there cannot be unification.

There never was any separation. Are you getting this?

Certainly, I feel in a super-aware state, where everything makes sense. It's good to be back in tune.

And what is your mission?

To re-unify, to joyously re-unify in a way that makes the reunification of others easier: to reunify with them to some degree along the way, and not just reunify with people, but reunify with animals, places, with the moment.

With the greater self. For the greater self is all these things. It is what it is looking at. It is what it is hearing. It is what it is touching. Truly it is.

In the greater self there is no separation.

All separation is illusion. All there is, is all there is, and there is nothing that is not.

So let me get this, I am what I see, but what I see is outside of me: so how can it be me too?

Me two: that's good. A part of your self is looking at another part of yourself, nothing else, me-one is looking at me-two. It's all me.

But that's you.

You become one with the oneness that is me when you lose your sense of a separate self and sense the oneness of everything.

But I cannot stand back from that and be the observer looking at the oneness all around me, for then there would be twoness: the observer and the observed.

You can feel it though, can't you?

A coherence that runs through everything, a permeating presence. My viewpoint is changing, I can observe my lesser self, the one who has the thoughts and emotions, but I am aware they aren't mine; they are only with me for a minute and then they are gone, they are just passing by. Even as the lesser self, I am the I who remains.

That is because you have a connection to the greater self.

As my connection to the greater self grows so my connection to the lesser self diminishes. And how do I do that?

Pay less attention to your lower self lesser self and pay more attention to the greater self.

But how do I know which is which?

You know perfectly well which is which. You can feel the difference.

The greater self is always reassuring, always loving, always affirming. The greater self knows everything is OK, that it is alright now, it always was and will be. The greater self has values that, deep down, we all subscribe to.

Because deep down, we are all the greater self.

We are going round in circles.

We are the circle. Another thing: spend more time with me, if you want to grow your consciousness of me. Enjoy my presence.

I do.

Be here more.

My response was going to be, I'm busy, I have so many things to do, but it isn't. the answer is, I will.

Because ...

Better awareness of you puts me in a better place where I have better answers for life's challenges. There was nothing else I wanted to do other than be your disciple.

You've wanted to do plenty of other things: you still do!

OK, yes, but it feels like, at another level of the self, there was nothing else I ever wanted to do, that everything else pales.

And then it brightens, and that is part of the experience of being you.

Surely that is part of the experience of not being me.

The lesser you, the greater, you, me, all are aspects of you.

You are an aspect of me.

How could I not be? You are in me and I am in you. You are an aspect of me and I am an aspect of you, stop thinking of us as separate. When you think you are sensing a God who is somewhere else, you are already not in unity.

Why do we think God is somewhere else?

You know that as soon as you do you have absolutely and completely missed me. If I am not in you, I am not God, isn't this obvious to you?

But we are taught to look up to God.

Don't look up to God, look into God. As soon as you look up to me, you are lost. Why do you overlook me?

When you think about it, it is as if we are missing everything, you, ourselves, everything. We have been looking in the wrong places.

You have not known who you are.

The Other Side of You

Here is the start of The Other Side of You.

≈

Tell me my truth

OK, I'll tell you

What is it?

It is you

I am my truth - that's it?

Who did you think you were?

Confused, I was confused

You hadn't discovered who you were

≈

OK, and now I have

No, you haven't

What?

You are still discovering who you are

Help me here

What do you think I am doing?

I know, I know

You know so little

≈

To find my truth I must find myself?
Find more of yourself
Not the self, the whole self and nothing but?
Life is a process of growth
Evolution - "Survival of the fittest"
Life for all, change for all
Death for all!
Everything changes - life survives

≈

I survive!
That depends who you think you are?
Get that wrong and I don't survive?
You change form
But I survive
You are a myth
What?
You don't exist

≈

Now I am nowhere – explain

You think of yourself as independent

I appreciate that we are interconnected

You don't really get that

What am I missing?

There is only being

And I am being me

That is an illusion

≈

So who am I being?

You have the experience of being you

But who am I really?

Us, there is only us

And what part of us am I missing?

Almost the whole thing

And how do I get that?

Know that you are not separate

≈

Printed in Great Britain
by Amazon

62496567R00088